BIRDS OF
GREAT BRITAIN
EUROPE & AFRICA

BIRDS OF
GREAT BRITAIN
EUROPE & AFRICA

AN ILLUSTRATED ENCYCLOPEDIA AND BIRDWATCHING GUIDE

DAVID ALDERTON

southwater

This edition is published by Southwater
Southwater is an imprint of Anness Publishing Ltd
Hermes House, 88–89 Blackfriars Road, London SE1 8HA
tel. 020 7401 2077; fax 020 7633 9499
www.southwaterbooks.com; info@anness.com
© Anness Publishing Ltd 2004

UK agent: The Manning Partnership Ltd; tel. 01225 478444;
fax 01225 478440; sales@manning-partnership.co.uk
UK distributor: Grantham Book Services Ltd; tel. 01476 541080;
fax 01476 541061; orders@gbs.tbs-ltd.co.uk
North American agent/distributor: National Book Network; tel. 301 459 3366;
fax 301 429 5746; www.nbnbooks.com
Australian agent/distributor: Pan Macmillan Australia; tel. 1300 135 113;
fax 1300 135 103; customer.service@macmillan.com.au
New Zealand agent/distributor: David Bateman Ltd; tel. (09) 415 7664; fax (09) 415 8892

Publisher: Joanna Lorenz
Editorial Director: Helen Sudell
Project Editors: Debra Mayhew and Catherine Stuart
Book and Jacket design: Nigel Partridge
Illustrators: see Picture Acknowledgements, below
Production Controller: Darren Price
Material in this book was previously published as part of a larger volume,
The World Encyclopedia of Birds & Birdwatching
1 3 5 7 9 10 8 6 4 2

PICTURE ACKNOWLEDGEMENTS

All photographs appearing on the cover were supplied by Dennis Avon.
Front cover, clockwise from left: red-billed hornbill (*Tocus erythrorhynchus*); common
redstart (*Phoenicurus Phoenicurus*); hoopoe (Upupa epops); barn owl (*Tyto alba*)
Back cover, from left: robin (*Erithacus rubecula*); kingfisher (*Ceryle alcyon*).

Pictures appearing on pages 1–5: page 1, greater-spotted woodpecker *(Picoides major)*;
page 2, cape sugarbird *(Promerops caper)*; page 3, merlin *(Falco columbarius)*;
page 4, grey heron *(Ardea cinerea)*; page 5T, rock partridge *(Alectoris graeca)*;
page 5B, orange weaver *(Euplectes orix)*.

The Publisher would like to thank
the following picture agencies for
granting permission to use their
photographs in this book:
Key: l = left, r = right, t = top,
m = middle, b = bottom
David Alderton: 27t, 56b,
Ardea: 6t, 11br, 12r, 13t, 13b, 17m,
17b, 18t, 19br, 21tr, 21b, 22b, 23b, 24t,
27b, 29t, 29m, 29b, 31m, 33b, 34, 35,
36t, 37t, 37m, 38t, 48tl, 48tr, 52t, 56m,
58t, 60t, 61tr, 66tl, 66tr.
Dennis Avon: 11ml, 11bl, 13m, 20bl,
21tl, 24bl, 25t, 25b, 30t, 48b, 50, 54,
58b, 60b.
Oxford Scientific Films: 6b, 9, 11tl,
11tr, 11mr, 12l, 16b, 22t, 23tl, 23tr,
24br, 26b, 28t, 31t, 33t, 37b, 38b, 39t,
39b, 41t, 41b, 42, 44t, 46t, 46br, 52b,
56t, 61tl, 61b.
All artwork by Peter Barrett except:
Anna Childs: 74, 75, 122, 123.
Anthony Duke: 40; all location maps,
pp66–125.
Studio Galante: 70, 71, 102, 106,
107, 112, 113.
Martin Knowelden: 8, 9, 10, 15, 17t,
18l, 19t, 20r, 26r, 28b.
Andrew Robinson: 92, 93.
Tim Thackeray: 68, 69, 76, 77, 78,
79, 80, 81, 82, 83, 84, 85, 86, 87,
90, 91, 110, 111, 116, 117, 118, 119,
124, 125.

CONTENTS

INTRODUCTION

Birds have been a source of fascination and inspiration to people since the dawn of history. Birds' mastery of the skies not only inspired humans to invent flying machines but also helped facilitate the development of modern aircraft, since aeroplane designers borrowed the aerodynamic features of birds to revolutionize intercontinental travel.

Birds have also influenced our cultures in a spiritual sense, as indicated, for example, by the thunderbird legends of the native North Americans and the phoenix featured in Egyptian mythology. In Europe also, birds have become significant in various festivals. The robin has become linked with Christmas, while the return of the common cuckoo (*Cuculus canorus*), from its African wintering grounds, is eagerly awaited as a sign of Spring. More unusually, the habit of nesting on rooftops favoured by white storks (*Ciconia ciconia*) enabled the parents of newborn babies to pretend to their curious children that the birds had carried them to the home.

It may seem surprising, but there are still new species of birds being discovered every year. Among the most recent is a new bald-headed parrot from the Mato Grosso region of Brazil, reported for the first time

Below: Birds have adapted to live, feed and breed in a wide range of different habitats. Here a puffin (Fratercula arctica) *is returning from a successful fishing trip at sea.*

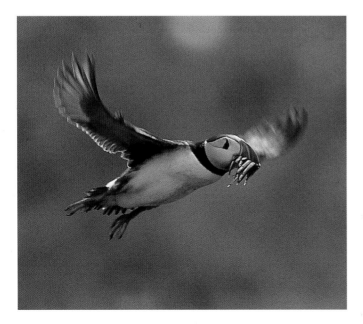

Above: The ostrich (Struthio camelus) *is the largest bird in the world today, and can be found in open countryside, mainly in central and southern parts of Africa. Its call has been likened to a lion's roar.*

in July 2002. As an approximate guide, there are over 9,000 avian species present on Earth – a total far in excess of the number of mammals. There is virtually no environment on the planet where birds are not to be seen, even in the freezing tundra of the Arctic, where auks such as puffins (*Fratercula arctica*) nest in underground burrows or cliff faces to incubate eggs in one of the most inhospitable regions on Earth.

Birds have spread so widely over the surface of the planet not only because of their ability to fly, but also because they are often highly adaptable in their dietary habits. Birds eat a wide variety of foods, ranging from microsopic plankton to the carcasses of large mammals, as well as all types of vegetable matter and numerous invertebrates.

In recent years, human activities have continued to take their toll on avian populations around the world, and are now threatening the very survival of many species. On the bright side, however, more positive intervention is seeking to right these wrongs by using thorough research to promote the survival of diminished populations. The current efforts to rear and relocate young golden eagles (*Aquila chrysaetos*), discussed later under Endangered Species and Conservation, is an encouraging example of this new enlightenment.

Birdwatching has also benefited from new advances, and media such as the Internet now enable valuable

Below: Advanced photographic equipment has greatly aided the study of birds, enabling species such as this hoopoe (Upupa epops) *to be observed in flight and even at the entrance to its nest.*

information on new sightings to be relayed instantly. Undoubtedly, webcam opportunities to observe bird sites, even on another continent, will increase in the years ahead. The fact that we are able to spot birds in any locality helps to explain why it remains a popular pastime. No special equipment is necessarily required, although binoculars, sketchpads and similar items can add to your enjoyment and understanding of avian life.

This book is a celebration of birds that sets out to reveal the diversity in both their form and lifestyles. The second part features a directory of species which can be seen throughout Great Britain, Europe and Africa, and off the shores of these continents. Each bird is placed within the geographical context in which it is most likely to be seen. Even if you do not have the opportunity to visit the forests of the Congo, or the icy landscape of the northern Arctic, you can still marvel at the diversity of avian life, as portrayed in these pages.

THE ORIGINS OF BIRDS

Vertebrates – first flying reptiles called pterosaurs, and later birds – took to the air about 190 million years ago. Adapting to an aerial existence marked a very significant step in vertebrate development, because of the need for a new method of locomotion, and a radically different body design.

The age of *Archaeopteryx*

Back in 1861, workers in a limestone quarry in Bavaria, southern Germany, unearthed a strange fossil that resembled a bird in appearance and was about the size of a modern crow, but also had teeth. The idea that the fossil was a bird was confirmed by the clear evidence of feathers impressed into the stone, as the presence of plumage is one of the characteristic distinguishing features of all birds. The 1860s were a time when the debate surrounding evolution was becoming fierce, and the discovery created huge interest, partly because it suggested that birds may have evolved from dinosaurs. It confirmed that birds had lived on Earth for at least 145 million years, existing even before the age of the dinosaurs came to a close in the Cretaceous period, about 65 million years ago. As the oldest-known bird, it was given the name *Archaeopteryx*, meaning "ancient wings".

Pterosaurs

A study of the anatomy of *Archaeopteryx*'s wings revealed that these early birds did not just glide but were capable of using their wings for active flight. Yet they were not the first vertebrate creatures to have taken to the skies. Pterosaurs had already successfully developed approximately 190 million years ago, during the Jurassic period, and even co-existed with birds for a time. In fact, the remains of one of the later pterosaurs, called *Rhamphorhynchus*, have been found in the same limestone deposits in southern Germany where *Archaeopteryx* was discovered. The pterosaur's wings more closely resembled those of a bat than a bird, consisting simply of a membrane supported by a bony framework, rather than feathers overlying the skin.

Some types of pterosaurs developed huge wingspans, in excess of 7m (23ft), which enabled them to glide almost effortlessly over the surface of the world's oceans, much like albatrosses do today. It appears that they fed primarily on fish and other marine life, scooping their food out of the water in flight. Changes in climate probably doomed the pterosaurs, however, since increasingly turbulent weather patterns meant that gliding became difficult, and they could no longer fly with ease.

Avian giants

In the period immediately after the extinction of the dinosaurs, some groups of birds increased rapidly in physical size, and in so doing, lost the ability to fly. Since their increased size meant that they could cover large distances on foot, and as they faced no predators, because large hunting mammals had not yet evolved, these large birds were relatively safe. In New Zealand, home of the large flightless moas, such giants thrived until the start of human settlement about a millennium ago. The exact date of the final extinction of the moas is not recorded, but the group had probably died out entirely by the middle of the 19th century.

Below: The largest species of moa would have dwarfed a man.

Right: An impression of how Archaeopteryx may have looked. It is impossible to be sure of the coloration from its fossilized remains.

Below: All pterosaurs had a similar body shape with a narrow head, which may have been embellished with a crest of some sort. This may have been used for display purposes and also to reduce air resistance in flight. The wing structure of pterosaurs was very different from that of birds: their wings basically consisted of skin membranes, stretched out behind the forearms.

It was this large surface area that allowed them to glide with little effort, but becoming airborne in the first place required great effort. The lack of body covering over the skin also had the effect of causing greater heat loss from the body. In birds, the feathers provide insulation as well as assisting active flight.

Below: The chicks of the South American hoatzin (Opisthocomus hoazin) are unique in possessing claws on their wing tips, which enable them to climb trees. These claws disappear by the time the birds are old enough to fly.

The spread of birds

After the age of *Archaeopteryx*, it is thought that birds continued to radiate out over the globe and became increasingly specialized. Unfortunately, there is very little fossil evidence to help us understand their early history. This lack of fossils is partly due to the fact that the small carcasses of birds would have been eaten whole by scavengers, and partly because their lightweight, fragile skeletons would not have fossilized easily. In addition, most birds would not have been trapped and died under conditions that were favourable for fossilization.

By the end of the age of the dinosaurs, birds had become far more numerous. Many seabirds still possessed teeth in their jaws, reflecting their reptilian origins. These probably assisted them in catching fish and other aquatic creatures. It was at this stage that the ancestors of contemporary bird groups such as waterfowl and gulls started to emerge. Most of the forerunners of today's birds had evolved by the Oligocene epoch, some 38 million years ago.

Some groups of birds that existed in these times have since disappeared, notably the phororhacids, which ranged widely over South America and even into parts of the southern United States. These birds were fearsome predators, capable of growing to nearly 3m (10ft) in height. They were equipped with deadly beaks and talons, and probably hunted together in groups.

Recent finds

During the mid-1990s, the discovery of avian fossils in China that were apparently contemporary with those of *Archaeopteryx* aroused considerable interest. Like its German relative, *Confuciusornis* possessed claws on the tips of its wings, which probably helped these early birds to move around. Similar claws are seen today in hoatzin chicks. *Confuciusornis* resembled modern birds more closely than *Archaeopteryx* in one significant respect: it lacked teeth in its jaws. Further study of the recent fossil finds from this part of the world is required, however, as some may not be genuine.

THE SKELETON AND PARTS OF A BIRD

The bird's skeleton has evolved to be light yet robust, both characteristics that help with flight. To this end, certain bones, particularly in the skull, have become fused, while others are absent, along with the teeth. The result is that birds' bodies are lightweight compared to those of other vertebrates.

In order to be able to fly, a bird needs a lightweight body so that it can become airborne with minimal difficulty. It is not just teeth that are missing from the bird's skull, but the associated heavy jaw muscles as well. These have been replaced by a light, horn-covered bill that is adapted in shape to the bird's feeding habits. Some of the limb bones, such as the humerus in the shoulder, are hollow, which also cuts down on weight. At the rear of the body, the bones in the vertebral column have become fused, which gives greater stability as well as support for the tail feathers.

The avian skeleton

In birds, the most marked evidence of specialization can be seen in the legs. Their location is critical to enable a bird to maintain its balance. The legs are found close to the midline, set slightly back near the bird's centre of gravity. These limbs are powerful, helping to provide lift at take-off and absorb the impact of landing. Strong legs also allow most birds to hop over the ground with relative ease.

There are some differences in the skeleton between different groups of birds. The atlas and axis bones at the start of the vertebral column are fused in the case of hornbills, for example, but in no other family.

Feet and toes

Birds' feet vary in length, and are noticeably extended in waders, which helps them to distribute their weight more evenly. The four toes may be arranged either in a typical 3:1 perching grip, with three toes gripping the front of the perch and one behind, or in a 2:2 configuration, known as zygodactyl, which gives a surer grip. The zygodactyl grip is seen in relatively few groups of birds, notably parrots and toucans. Touracos have flexible toes so they can swap back and forth between these two options.

The zygodactyl arrangement of their toes helps some parrots to use their feet like hands for holding food. Birds generally have claws at the ends of their toes, which have developed into sharp talons in the case of birds of prey, helping them to catch their quarry even in flight. Many birds also use their claws for preening, and they can provide balance for birds that run or climb.

Right: The typical skeleton of a bird. Note the prominent breastbone for the attachment of flight muscles. The large area occupied by the orbit of the eye reflects the fact that birds in general rely heavily on their sense of sight.

Parrot

Above: Parrots use their feet for holding food, rather like human hands.

Bird of prey

Above: In birds of prey, the claws have become talons for grasping prey.

Wader

Above: Long toes make it easier for waders to walk over muddy ground or water plants.

Duck

Above: The webbed feet of ducks provide propulsion in water.

1 Metacarpals
2 Alula
3 Ulna
4 Radius
5 Cervical vertebrae
6 Ear
7 Cranium
8 Eye socket
9 Nostril
10 Bill (upper mandible)
11 Bill (lower mandible)
12 Clavicle (wishbone)
13 Ribs
14 Sternum (breastbone)
15 Metatarsals
16 Tarsus
17 Tibia and Fibula
18 Femur
19 Humerus

Above: The narrow bill of waders such as this curlew (Numenius arquata) enables these birds to probe for food in sandy or muddy areas.

Above: Birds of prey such as the golden eagle (Aquila chrysaetos) rely on a sharp bill with a hooked tip to tear their prey apart.

Above: Herons (Ardea) have strong, pointed bills, which they use like scissors to seize and hold slippery prey such as frogs.

Above: Flamingos (Phoenicopteridae) have bills that enable them to feed with their heads trailing backwards in the water.

Above: The grey parrot (Psittacus erithacus) has a strong bill for cracking nuts, further aided by a pointed tip on the upper part.

Above: Whale-headed storks (Balaeniceps rex) have large bills that allow them to scoop up quite large vertebrate prey.

Bills

The bills of birds vary quite widely in shape and size, and reflect their feeding habits. The design of the bill also has an impact on the force that it can generate. The bills of many larger parrots are especially strong, allowing them to crack hard nut shells. In addition, they can move their upper and lower bill independently, which produces a wider gape and, in turn, allows more pressure to be exerted.

Wings

A bird's wing is built around just three digits, which correspond to human fingers. In comparison, bats have five digits supporting their fleshy membranes. The three digits of birds provide a robust structure. The power of the wings is further enhanced by the fusion of the wrist bones and the carpals to create the single bone known as the carpometacarpus, which runs along the rear of the wing.

At the front of the chest, the clavicles are joined together to form what in chickens is called the wishbone. The large, keel-shaped breastbone, or sternum, runs along the underside of the body. It is bound by the ribs to the backbone, which provides stability, especially during flight. In addition, the major flight muscles are located in the lower body when the bird is airborne.

Bizarrely built birds

Nature has resulted in a number of decidedly odd-looking birds, notably on the offshore islands of vast oceans where they evolved undisturbed by predators. One famous species has captured the human imagination for centuries. First recorded in 1601, the dodo (*Raphus cucullatus*) had been driven to extinction by 1690, although several living examples of this flightless pigeon were brought to Europe, and aroused great curiosity because of their ungainly appearance. Unfortunately, many of today's representations of dodos are the subject of some artistic licence, as there is not a complete surviving specimen in any museum in the world. Those on display at such institutions have been constructed with reference to contemporary accounts and artworks, and it has been noted by ornithologists that, while early European portraits capture the dodo's athleticism, later artworks increasingly depict the famous bird as fat, colourful and ungainly. This may, in part, suggest a preference for the absurd among the artists, but also that the captive dodos were fed an inappropriate diet. These portraits should not be viewed as a measure of strict anatomical accuracy.

Below: The most striking feature of the dodo was its long, hooked bill. As a flightless bird, its wings were little more than stubs which hung on each side of its plump body. Rather uniquely, it also seems to have possessed a short tail. The legs, by contrast, were thick and strong – a valuable support for its weight, and possibly also an aid to speed and agility when running through woodland.

FEATHERS

The presence of feathers is one of the main distinguishing characteristics that set birds apart from other groups of creatures on the planet. The number of feathers on a bird's body varies considerably – a swan may have as many as 25,000 feathers, for instance, while a tiny hummingbird has just 1,000 in all.

Aside from the bill, legs and feet, the entire body of the bird is covered in feathers. The plumage does not grow randomly over the bird's body, but develops along lines of so-called feather tracts, or pterylae. These are separated by bald areas known as apteria. The apteria are not conspicuous under normal circumstances, because the contour feathers overlap to cover the entire surface of the body. Plumage may also sometimes extend down over the legs and feet as well, in the case of birds from cold climates, providing extra insulation here.

Feathers are made of a tough protein called keratin, which is also found in our hair and nails. Birds have three main types of feathers: the body, or contour, feathers; the strong, elongated flight feathers on the wings, and the warm, wispy down feathers next to their skin.

A diet deficient in sulphur-containing amino acids, which are the basic building blocks of protein, will result in poor feathering, creating "nutritional barring" across the flight and tail feathers. Abnormal plumage coloration can also have nutritional causes in some cases. These changes are usually reversible if more favourable environmental conditions precede the next moult.

The functions of feathers

Plumage has a number of functions, not just relating to flight. It provides a barrier that retains warm air close to the bird's body and helps to maintain body temperature, which is higher in birds than mammals – typically between 41 and 43.5°C (106 and 110°F). The down feathering that lies close to the skin, and the overlying contour plumage, are vital for maintaining body warmth. Most birds have a small volume relative to their surface area, which can leave them vulnerable to hypothermia.

A special oil produced by the preen gland, located at the base of the tail, waterproofs the plumage. This oil, which is spread over the feathers as the bird preens itself, prevents water penetrating the feathers, which would cause the bird to become so

Below: Feathering is highly significant for display purposes in some species, particularly members of the Phasanidae family. The cock blue peafowl (Pavo cristatus) has a very elaborate train of feathers, which it fans open to deter rivals and attract mates.

Above: A bird's flight feathers are longer and more rigid than the contour feathers that cover the body, or the fluffy down feathers that lie next to the skin. The longest, or primary, flight feathers, which generate most thrust, are located along the outer rear edges of the wings. The tail feathers are often similar in shape to the flight feathers, with the longest being found in the centre. Splaying the tail feathers increases drag and so slows the bird down.

1 Primaries
2 Secondaries
3 Axillaries
4 Rump
5 Lateral tail feathers
6 Central tail feathers
7 Breast
8 Cere

9 Auricular region (ear)
10 Nape
11 Back
12 Greater under-wing coverts
13 Lesser under-wing coverts

Above: The vulturine guineafowl (Acryllium vulturinum) *is so-called because of its bare head and neck, which is a feature of vultures, although it is not a carnivorous species itself.*

waterlogged that it could no longer fly. The contour feathers that cover the body are also used for camouflage in many birds. Barring, in particular, breaks up the outline of the bird's body, helping to conceal it in its natural habitat.

The plumage has become modified in some cases, reflecting the individual lifestyle of the species concerned. Woodpeckers, for example, have tail feathers that are short and rather sharp at their tips, providing additional support for gripping onto the sides of trees. Vultures, on the other hand, have bare heads because plumage here would soon become stained and matted with blood when these birds fed on a carcass.

Social significance of plumage

Plumage can also be important in social interactions between birds. Many species have differences in their feathering that separate males from females, and often juveniles can also be distinguished by their plumage. Cock birds are usually more brightly coloured, which helps them to attract their mates, but this does not apply in every case. The difference between the sexes in terms of their plumage can be quite marked. Cock birds of a number

of species have feathers forming crests as well as magnificent tail plumes, which are seen to greatest effect in peacocks (*Pavo cristatus*), whose display is one of the most remarkable sights in the whole of the avian world.

Recent studies have confirmed that the birds that appear relatively dull in colour to our eyes, such as the hill mynah (*Gracula religiosa*) with its blackish plumage, are seen literally in a different light by other birds. They are able to visually perceive the ultraviolet component of light, which is normally invisible to us, making these seemingly dull birds appear greener. Ultraviolet coloration may also be significant in helping birds to choose their mates.

Moulting

Birds' feathering is maintained by preening, but it becomes frayed and worn over time. It is therefore replaced by new plumage during the process of moulting, when the old feathers are shed. Moulting is most often an annual event. However, many young birds shed their nest feathers before they are a year old.

Moulting may also be triggered by the onset of the breeding season in some species, as is the case in many whydahs and weavers. These birds resemble sparrows for much of the year, but their appearance is transformed at the onset of the breeding period. Whydah cock birds develop lengthy tail plumes, and the birds also become more strikingly coloured. Hormonal alterations in the body are important in triggering this process, with external factors such as changing day length also playing a part.

Iridescence

Some birds are not brightly coloured, but their plumage literally sparkles in the light, thanks to its structure, which creates an iridescent effect. One of the particular features of iridescence is that the colour of the plumage alters, depending on the angle at which it is viewed, often appearing quite dark, almost black from a side view. This phenomenon is particularly common in some groups of birds, notably members of the starling family (Sturnidae), hummingbirds (Trochilidae) and sunbirds (Nectarinidae), which are described as having metallic feathers as a result.

In some cases, the iridescent feathering is localized, while in others, it is widespread over most of the body. Green and blue iridescence is common, with reddish sheens being seen less often. Iridescence is especially common in cock birds, helping them to attract mates. In some cases, therefore, it is seen only in the breeding plumage, notably on the upperparts of the body and the wings rather than the underparts.

Below: Many cock sunbirds, such as this West African green-headed species (Nectarinia verticalis), *display green or bluish iridescent plumage on the head.*

Right: The feather shaft holds the feather in place in the skin. The barbs run off the shaft at regular intervals, rather like the branches of a tree, and divide into smaller branches called barbules. These have tiny hooks attached to them that reinforce the structure of the flight feather, making it more rigid.

Barb Barbule

Shaft

FLIGHT

Some birds spend much of their lives in the air, whereas others will only fly as a last resort if threatened. A few species are too heavy to take off at all. The mechanics of flight are similar in all birds, but flight patterns vary significantly, which can help to identify the various groups in the air.

In most cases, the whole structure of the bird's body has evolved to facilitate flight. It is important for a bird's body weight to be relatively light, because this lessens the muscular effort required to keep it airborne. The powerful flight muscles, which provide the necessary lift, can account for up to a third of the bird's total body weight. They are attached to the breastbone, or sternum, in the midline of the body, and run along the sides of the body from the clavicle along the breastbone to the top of the legs.

Weight and flight

There is an upper weight limit of just over 18kg (40lb), above which birds would not be able to take off successfully. Some larger birds, notably pelicans and swans, need a run-up in order to gain sufficient momentum to lift off, particularly from water. Smaller birds can dart straight off a perch. Approaching the critical upper weight limit for flight, the male Kori bustard (*Ardeotis kori*) is the world's heaviest flying bird, although it prefers to run rather than fly because of the effort involved in becoming airborne.

Below: A typical take-off, as shown by a Harris's hawk (Parabuteo unicinctus).

Above: Birds such as the lammergeier or bearded vulture (Gypaetus barbatus) can remain airborne with minimum expenditure of energy, by gliding rather than flying.

Wing shape and beat

The shape of the wing is important for a bird's flying ability. Birds that remain airborne for much of their lives, such as albatrosses, have relatively long wings that allow them to glide with relatively little effort. The wandering albatross (*Diomedea exulans*) has the largest wingspan of any bird, measuring about 3.4m (11ft) from one wing tip to the other. Large, heavy birds such as griffon vultures (*Gyps fulvus*) may have difficulty in flying early in the day, before the land has warmed up. This is because at this stage, there is insufficient heat coming up from the ground to create the thermal air currents that help to keep them airborne. In common with other large birds of prey, griffon vultures seek out these rising columns of air, which provide uplift, and then circle around in them.

The number of wing beats varies dramatically between different species. Hummingbirds (Trochilidae), for example, beat their wings at a greater frequency than any other bird as they hover in front of flowers. Their wings move so fast – sometimes at over 200 beats per minute – that they appear as a total blur to our eyes. At the other extreme, heavy birds such as swans fly with slow, deliberate wing beats.

Lightening the load

It is not just the lightness of the bird's skeleton that helps it to fly. There have been evolutionary changes in the body organs too, most noticeably in the urinary system. Unlike mammals, birds do not have a bladder that fills with urine. Instead, their urine is greatly concentrated, in the form of uric acid, and passes out of the body with their faeces, appearing as a creamy-white, semi-solid component.

1. When resting, a bird typically has a relatively upright stance.

2. As it leans forwards for take-off, it raises its wings and starts to lift its legs.

3. Leaving its perch, the bird pushes off into the air, and opens its wings.

Above: Waterfowl such as this mallard (Anas platyrhynchos) have few difficulties becoming airborne from water, as their plumage is designed to prevent waterlogging.

Below: Some gulls (Laridae) spend much of their lives on the wing, scanning the surface of the ocean for a sign of prey.

The aerofoil principle

Once in flight, the shape of the wing is crucial in keeping the bird airborne. Viewed in cross-section from the side, a bird's wing resembles an aeroplane's wing, called an aerofoil, and in fact aeroplanes use the same technique as birds to fly.

The wing is curved across the top, so the movement of air is faster over this part of the wing compared with the lower surface. This produces reduced air pressure on top of the wing, which provides lift and makes it easier for the bird to stay in the air.

The long flight feathers at the rear edge of the wings help to provide the thrust and lift for flight. The tail feathers, too, can help the bird remain airborne. The kestrel (*Falco tinnunculus*), for example, having spotted prey on the ground, spreads its tail feathers to help it remain aloft while it hovers to target its prey.

A bird's wings move in a regular figure-of-eight movement while it is in flight. During the downstroke, the flight feathers join together to push powerfully against the air. The primary flight feathers bend backwards, which propels the bird forwards. As the wing moves upwards, the longer primary flight feathers move apart, which reduces air resistance. The secondary feathers further along the wing provide some slight propulsion. After that the cycle repeats itself.

Above: The flow of air over a bird's wing varies according to the wing's position.
1. When the wing is stretched out horizontally, an area of low pressure is created above the wing, causing lift.
2. As the wing is tilted downwards, the flow of the air is disrupted, causing turbulence and loss of lift.
3. When the wing is angled downwards, lift slows, which results in stalling. The bird's speed slows as a consequence.

Flight patterns and formations

Different species of birds have various ways of flying, which can actually aid the birdwatcher in helping to identify them. For example, small birds such as tits (Paridae) and finches (Fringillidae) alternately flap their wings and fold them at their sides, adopting a streamlined shape, which helps to save energy. This produces a characteristic dipping flight. Larger birds such as ducks and geese (Anatidae) maintain a straighter course at an even height.

In some cases, it is not just the individual flying skills of a bird that can help it to stay airborne, but those of its fellows nearby. Birds flying in formation create a slipstream, which makes flying less effort for all the birds behind the leader. This formation is often used on long-distance journeys.

4. Powerful upward and downward sweeps of the wings propel the bird forwards.

5. When coming in to land, a bird lowers its legs and slows its wing movements.

6. Braking is achieved by a vertical landing posture, with the tail feathers spread.

LOCOMOTION

For most birds, flight is the main means of locomotion. However, the ability to move on the ground or in water can be vital, particularly when it comes to obtaining food. Some birds have even lost the ability to fly, relying instead on their swimming or running skills to escape predators and find food.

Not all birds possess the ability to fly, but this does not mean they are handicapped in their natural environment. Penguins may appear to be rather clumsy shuffling around on land, but they are extremely well adapted to life in the water. Like other primarily aquatic birds, their webbed feet enable them to swim very effectively. Webbing is a common feature seen in aquatic birds. The skin folds linking the toes turn the foot into an effective paddle, allowing the bird to maximize its propulsive forward thrust by pushing against the water. On land, however, webbed feet do impose certain restrictions, because being linked together in this way means that the individual toes are not as flexible.

Aquatic locomotion
When penguins dive, their sleek, torpedo-shaped bodies allow them to swim fast underwater, reaching speeds equivalent to 40km/h (25mph). Their flippers, which evolved from wings,

Below: A group of king penguins (Aptenodytes patagonicus) *leap in and out of the water as they swim along, in a form of movement known as porpoising.*

help them to steer very effectively as they pursue fish, which form the basis of their diet. Like flying birds, penguins need effective wing muscles to control their movements, so their skeletal structure bears a close similarity to that of flying birds.

Flightless ducks and other aquatic birds, such as the Galapagos Island cormorant (*Nannopterum harrisi*), use a different method of locomotion: they rely entirely on their feet rather than their wings for propulsive power. Their skeletons differ from those of flying birds in that they lack the prominent keel on the sternum for the attachment of flight muscles.

Flightless land birds
A number of land birds have lost the ability to fly. Typically, they are birds that inhabit islands where, until the arrival of cats and rats brought by ships from Europe, they faced few predators. The arrival of predators has left them vulnerable, and many have since become extinct, including the dodo (*Raphus cucullatus*) – a large, flightless pigeon from the island of Mauritius in the Indian Ocean. Even larger in stature was the elephant bird

Above: Puffins (Fratercula arctica) *are less agile on land than they are in the sea, and spend much of their life in the water. When swimming, they use their wings like flippers.*

(*Aepyornis maximis*), a gigantic species found on Madagascar until as recently as 400 years ago. These birds would dwarf a modern ostrich in size, standing up to 3.15m (10ft) tall, and weighing perhaps as much as 454kg (1,000lb). Their eggs had a volume comparable to seven ostrich eggs, and measured over 30cm (12in) in length.

The moas (*Dinornis maximus*) of New Zealand were the most diverse group of flightless birds ever recorded, the last examples dying out in the 19th century, around the time of European settlement. There may have been as many as a dozen or more different species, and they filled the same sort of niche as grazing mammals, which were then absent from New Zealand.

In the absence of predatory mammals, the moas faced no significant threats to their survival until the first human settlers reached New Zealand. Their large size made them conspicuous, and, having evolved in an environment where they had been safe from persecution, they had lost their ability to fly. Moas were not even able to run fast, in contrast to modern flightless birds such as ostriches. Tragically, they were soon hunted to extinction.

Circulation

The circulatory system is vital in supporting the activities of both flighted and flightless birds, ensuring that their muscles are well supplied with oxygen. The heart acts as the pump, driving the blood around the body. The basic design of the heart is similar to that of a mammal, with the left side being highly developed because it does more work. Overall, the heart rate of birds is much more rapid than mammals of similar size, having been measured at 1,000 beats per minute in the case of canaries at rest. The heart beat rises dramatically during flight, but soon returns to normal when the bird touches down.

The respiratory system

Birds have lungs, located close to the vertebral column, but these do not expand and contract in the same way as those of mammals. Instead, birds rely on a series of air sacs that act rather like bellows, to suck

air through their respiratory system. In some cases, these link with the hollow limb bones, and thus help to meet the bird's high requirement for oxygen when flying. A bird's respiratory rate is a reflection of its body size, as well as its level of activity and lifestyle. Common starlings (*Sturnus vulgaris*), for example, typically breathe about 85 times every minute, whereas domestic chickens, which are more sedentary, have an equivalent respiratory rate of only about 20 breaths per minute.

1 Trachea
2 Interclavicular air sac
3 Lungs
4 Abdominal air sac
5 Femur (leg bone)
6 Cervical air sac
7 Humerus (wing bone)
8 Anterior thoracic air sac
9 Posterior thoracic air sac

Above: The ostrich (Struthio camelus) *is the only bird to have just two toes on each foot. This arrangement promotes stability when running, rather like a horse's hoof.*

Ratites

Not all flightless birds are helpless in the face of danger, however. The large, flightless birds known as ratites, including cassowaries, ostriches, emus and rheas, are particularly well able to defend themselves. Their strong legs are quite capable of inflicting lethal blows, especially in the case of the cassowaries (Casuariidae), found in parts of northern Australia, New Guinea and neighbouring islands. These birds have an elongated and deadly sharp claw on their innermost toe. If the cassowary is cornered and unable to run away, it lashes out with its legs and is quite capable of disembowelling a person with its

claws. The bird also has a hard, bony crest called a casque, which protects the top of its head.

The large ratites all share a similar shape, having bulky bodies, long legs and long, slender necks. Like all flightless birds, they do possess wings, which assist them in keeping their balance and may also be used for display purposes. Most birds have four toes on each foot, but ratites have no more than three toes, and less in some cases. Ostriches have just two toes on each foot. The fastest birds on land, they can run at speeds equivalent to 50km/h (31mph). The reduction in the number of toes may help these birds to run faster.

Emus (*Dromaius novaehollandiae*) have the most rudimentary wings of all ratites, which are not even used for display purposes. The rheas (Rheidae) of South America have the most prominent wings of the ratites. They cover the rump, but they do not enable these birds to fly, even when they are young.

Kiwis (Apterygidae) are also ratites, but they are much smaller birds with shorter legs. Unlike other ratites, they are not fast runners, but rely on camouflage and their nocturnal habits to conceal their presence from predators, rather than speed to escape.

Running in flighted birds

Some birds that are able to fly still prefer to use their running abilities to obtain food and escape danger. They include the roadrunners (*Geococcyx californianus*) of North America. With their short wings, these birds can fly clumsily, but prefer to use their strong legs to overtake and pounce on prey. In general, flying uses considerable energy compared to running or hopping. Many birds will elect to move swiftly over the ground to pounce on a food item or avoid an enemy if they judge that the situation does not warrant flight.

Above: The height and keen eyesight of ostriches means that they are hard to ambush in open country. Their pace allows them to escape from danger with little difficulty, while their long stride length when running enables them to cover large amounts of ground in a single step.

AVIAN SENSES

The keen senses of birds are vital to their survival, in particular helping them to find food, escape from enemies and find mates in the breeding season. Sight is the primary sense for most birds, but some species rely heavily on other senses to thrive in particular habitats.

All birds' senses are adapted to their environment, and the shape of their bodies can help to reflect which senses are most significant to them.

Sight and lifestyle

Most birds rely on their sense of sight to avoid danger, hunt for food and locate familiar surroundings. The importance of this sense is reflected by the size of their eyes, with those of

Field of vision

The positioning of a bird's eyes on its head affects its field of vision. The eyes of owls are positioned to face forwards, producing an overlapping image of the area in front known as binocular vision. This allows the owl to pinpoint its prey exactly, so that it can strike. In contrast, the eyes of birds that are likely to be preyed upon, such as woodcocks, are positioned on the sides of the head. This eye position gives a greatly reduced area of binocular vision, but it does give these birds practically all-round vision, enabling them to spot danger from all sides.

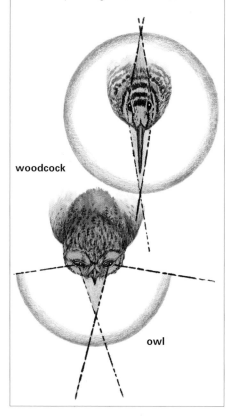

woodcock

owl

starlings (*Sturnus vulgaris*), for example, making up 15 per cent of the total head weight. The enlargement of the eyeballs and associated structures, notably the eye sockets in the skull, has altered the shape of the brain. In addition, the optic lobes in the brain, which are concerned with vision, are also enlarged, whereas the olfactory counterparts, responsible for smell, are poorly developed.

The structure of the eye also reveals much about a bird's habits. Birds of prey have large eyes in proportion to their head, and have correspondingly keen eyesight. Species that regularly hunt for prey underwater, such as penguins, can see well in the water. They have a muscle in each eye that reduces the diameter of the lens and increases its thickness on entering water, so that their eyes can adjust easily to seeing underwater. In addition, certain diving birds such as little auks (*Alle alle*) use a lens that forms part of the nictitating membrane, or third eyelid, which is normally hidden from sight. Underwater, when this membrane covers the eye, its convex shape serves as a lens, helping the bird to see in these surroundings.

Eye position

The positioning of the eyes on the head gives important clues to a bird's lifestyle. Most birds' eyes are set on the sides of the head. Owls, however, have flattened faces and forward-facing eyes that are critical to their hunting ability. These features allow owls to target their prey.

There are disadvantages, though – owls' eyes do not give a rounded view of the world, so they must turn their heads to see around them. It is not just the positioning of owls' eyes that is unusual. They are also able to hunt effectively in almost complete darkness. This is made possible in two

Above: Scavengers such as this lappet-faced vulture (Torgos tracheliotus) *have an acute sense of smell, and a huge beak that enables them to cut into the flesh of the carcass.*

ways. First, their pupils are large, which maximizes the amount of light passing through to the retina behind the lens, where the image is formed. Second, the cells here consist mainly of rods rather than cones. While cones give good colour vision, rods function to create images when background illumination is low.

The positioning of the eyes of game birds such as woodcocks (*Scolopax rusticola*) allows them to spot danger from almost any angle. It is even possible for them to see a predator sneaking up from behind. Their only blind spot is just behind the head.

Smell

Very few birds have a sense of smell, but kiwis (Apterygidae) and vultures (forming part of the order Falciformes) are notable exceptions. Birds' nostrils are normally located above the bill, opening directly into the skull, but kiwis' nostrils are positioned right at the end of the long bill. They probably help these birds to locate earthworms

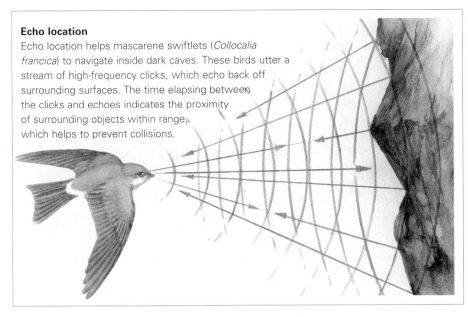

Echo location

Echo location helps mascarene swiftlets (*Collocalia francica*) to navigate inside dark caves. These birds utter a stream of high-frequency clicks, which echo back off surrounding surfaces. The time elapsing between the clicks and echoes indicates the proximity of surrounding objects within range, which helps to prevent collisions.

in the soil. Vultures have very keen eyesight, which helps them to spot dead animals on the ground from the air, but they also have a strong sense of smell, which helps when homing in on a distant carcass.

Taste

The senses of smell and taste are linked, and most birds also have correspondingly few taste buds in their mouths. The number of taste buds varies, with significant differences between groups of birds. Pigeons may have as few as 50 taste buds in their mouths, parrots as many as 400.

Birds' taste buds are located all around the mouth, rather than just on the tongue, as in mammals. The close

Below: Birds have good colour vision. It is this sense that enables sunbirds (Nectarinidae) to source nectar and pollen from these brightly-coloured red flowers.

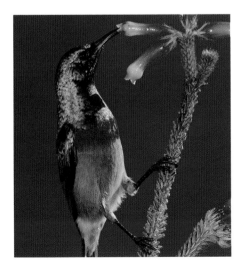

links between smell and taste can lead vultures, which feed only on fresh carcasses, to reject decomposing meat. They may start to eat it, but then spit it out once it is in their mouths, probably because of a combination of bad odour and taste.

Hearing

Birds generally do not have a highly developed sense of hearing. They lack any external ear flaps that would help to pinpoint sources of sound. The openings to their hearing system are located on the sides of the head, back from the eyes.

Hearing is of particular significance for nocturnal species, such as owls, which find their food in darkness. These birds are highly attuned to the calls made by rodents. The broad shape of their skull has the additional advantage of spacing the ear openings more widely, which helps them to localize the source of the sounds with greater accuracy.

Hearing is also important to birds during the breeding season. Birds show particular sensitivity to sounds falling within the vocal range of their chicks, which helps them to locate their offspring easily in the critical early days after fledging.

The Mascarene swiftlet *(Collocalia francica)*, which occurs on islands in the Indian Ocean east of Madagascar., uses echo location to find its way around in the dark, rather like bats do.

Unlike bats, however, the clicking sounds of the swiftlet's calls – up to 20 a second in darkness – are clearly audible to humans. The bird interprets the echoes of its call to avoid colliding with objects in its path, although it also uses its eyesight when flying. Cave swiftlets (*Aerodramus*) from Asia and the South American oilbird (*Steatornis caripensis*) navigate in a similar way.

Touch

The sense of touch is more developed in some birds than others. Those such as snipe (*Gallinago*), which have long bills for seeking food, have sensitive nerve endings called corpuscles in their bills that pick up tiny vibrations caused by their prey. Vibrations that could suggest approaching danger can also register via other corpuscles located particularly in the legs, so that the bird has a sensory awareness even when it is resting on a branch.

Wind-borne sensing

Tubenoses such as albatrosses and petrels (Procellariiformes) have a valve in each nostril that fills with air as the bird flies. These are affected by both the bird's speed and the wind strength. The valves almost certainly act as a type of wind gauge, allowing these birds to detect changes in wind strength and patterns. This information helps to keep them airborne, as they skim over the waves with minimal effort.

Below: A combination of senses, especially touch, helps oystercatchers (Haematopus ostralegus) to detect their prey, which is normally hidden from view.

PLANT-EATERS

All over the world, many birds depend on plant matter as part of their diet, with seeds and nuts in particular providing nourishment. A close relationship between plants and birds exists in many cases. Birds fertilize flowers when feeding on nectar, and help to spread their seeds when eating fruit.

Many different types of birds are primarily plant-eaters, whether feeding on flowers, fruit, nuts and seeds, or other plant matter. Plant-eating species have to eat a large volume of food compared to meat-eating species, because of the low nutritional value of plants compared with that of prey such as invertebrates.

In the last century or so, many species have benefited from the spread of agriculture, which now provides them with large acreages of suitable crop plants to feed on. These birds' feeding habits bring them into conflict with farmers when they breed rapidly in response to a swift expansion in their food supply. Across Africa, large populations of red-billed queleas (*Quelea quelea*) descend to feed on fields of wheat, sorghum and barley, resulting in a devastating loss of grain

Below: African touracos such as this red-crested species (Tauraco erythrolophus) are among the relatively few birds to feed on leaves. The touracos swallow these whole, and use a variable perching grip to maintain balance while feeding, even on thin branches.

and flattening of ripening plants. They have been labelled as pests, and are increasingly being culled by pesticides. This has led to an outbreak of protest from those who argue that the arable fields have actually replaced the birds' natural food sources.

Adapting to changing seasons

Birds from temperate areas exist on a varied diet that is related to the seasons. Bullfinches (*Pyrrhula pyrrhula*), for example, eat the buds in apple orchards in spring – when they can become a pest – while later in the year, they consume seeds and fruit. Their bills, like those of most other members of the finch family, are stout and relatively conical, which helps them to crack seeds effectively.

Some birds store plant food when it is plentiful, to sustain them through the winter. Nutcrackers (*Nucifraga*) collect hazel nuts, which they feed on through winter into the following year. Some woodpeckers (Picidae) drill holes in trees which they fill with acorns and other nuts and seeds, creating an easily accessible larder for the winter months, when snow may cover the ground.

Flowers

A number of birds rely on flowers rather than the whole plant as a source of food. Pollen is a valuable source of protein, while nectar provides sugars. Not surprisingly, flower-feeders tend to be confined to mainly tropical areas, where flowers are in bloom throughout the year. Hummingbirds (Trochilidae), for instance, use their narrow bills to probe into flowers to obtain nectar. Some hummingbirds have developed especially curved or elongated bills, which allow them to feed on particular flowers. These birds help to pollinate the plants on which they feed by transferring pollen from flower to flower on their bills or even on plumage.

The digestive system

Birds lack teeth, so their food must be swallowed whole. Birds have a storage organ known as the crop, which is located at the base of the neck. From here, food passes down into the proventriculus, where the digestive process starts, before entering the gizzard, which is equivalent to the mammalian stomach. Nutrients are then absorbed through the wall of the small intestine.

The digestive system of plant-eaters differs in various respects from that of predatory species. Vegetable matter is less nourishing than meat, so plant-eaters generally need longer digestive tracts to process the large quantities of food they must consume in order to obtain enough nourishment. In addition, digesting plant matter poses certain difficulties. The gizzards of seed-eating species such as many finches (Fringillidae) have especially thick muscular walls, which serve to grind up the seeds.

1 Oesophagus	6 Large intestine
2 Crop	7 Liver
3 Proventriculus	8 Spleen
4 Pancreas	9 Small intestine
5 Gizzard	

Above: Berries feature prominently in the diet of the pied barbet (Lybius leucomelas) – *their stocky bill allows these birds to pluck fruits easily from their stems. However, as opportunistic feeders, they will also eat other items, including invertebrates.*

The sunbirds (Nectarinidae) of Africa fill a similar evolutionary niche to America's hummingbirds, which they resemble in their small size and bright, often iridescent plumage. Unlike hummingbirds, however, they are not sufficiently agile to feed in flight, but have to perch within reach of the flower. Various members of the parrot family also feed on flowers. Their tongues are ideally equipped for this diet, with microscopic, bristle-like projections called papillae, which enable them to collect pollen easily.

Fruit

Exclusively frugivorous (fruit-eating) birds such as fruit doves (*Ptilinopus*) are found only in the tropics, where fruit is available throughout the year. These species usually dwell in tropical rainforests, where they have a valuable role to play in protecting the biodiversity of the forest. The seeds of the fruits they eat pass right through their digestive tracts unharmed, to be deposited far from the parent plant, which helps the plants to spread.

Plant matter

Relatively few birds feed almost entirely on herbage, although the bizarre hoatzin (*Opisthocomus hoazin*) from the rainforest of South America is one example. Equally unusual are the touracos (Musophagidae) of Africa, which also feed mainly on leaves, which they pluck along with fruits. Some parrots such as the eclectus (*Eclectus roratus*) are also believed to feed largely on plant matter rather than seeds or fruit.

The breakdown of vegetation presents considerable difficulty, since birds do not possess the necessary enzymes to digest the cellulose in plants. Birds such as grouse (Tetraonidae), which feed regularly on plant matter, have evolved long, blind-ending tubes known as caeca. These contain beneficial microbes that can break down cellulose.

Nuts and seeds

These dry foods are an invaluable resource to many different types of birds, ranging from parrots to finches. However, cracking the tough outer shell or husk can be a problem. Finches such as grosbeaks have evolved a particularly strong bill for this purpose. Hawfinches (*Coccothraustes coccothraustes*) are able to crack cherry stones (pits) to extract the kernel.

Above: Red-billed queleas, or weavers (Quelea quelea), *are the most numerous birds in the world. Massive flocks of these birds will wipe out crops of ripening millets in parts of Africa, to the extent that they are sometimes called "feathered locusts".*

The most bizarre example of bill adaption for eating seeds is seen in the crossbills (*Loxia*) of northern coniferous forests. These birds have literally twisted upper and lower mandibles, which help them to crack open the seeds inside the larch cones, which they eat. Some cockatoos such as the Moluccan species (*Cacatua moluccensis*) have bills that are even strong enough to open coconuts.

Below: Pink-footed geese (Anser brachyrhynchus) *can be a problem in agricultural areas, since they will sometimes descend in large numbers to graze on young cereal crops.*

PREDATORS AND SCAVENGERS

Just as with other vertebrates, there is a food chain within the avian kingdom. Some species hunt only other birds, while others seek a more varied range of prey, including, commonly, invertebrates. Even birds that feed mainly on seeds catch protein-rich insects to feed their chicks in the nest.

Some birds are active predators, seeking and killing their own food, while others prefer to scavenge on carcasses. Many predatory birds are opportunistic feeders, hunting when food is plentiful but scavenging in times of scarcity. Both hunters and scavengers have evolved to live in a wide range of environments, and display correspondingly diverse hunting skills to obtain their food.

Birds of prey have sharp bills that enable them to tear the flesh of their prey into strips small enough to swallow. Eating whole animals can potentially cause digestive problems for these birds because of the bones, skin, feathers and other relatively indigestible body parts. Owls overcome this problem by regurgitating pellets composed of the indigestible remains of their prey. Kingfishers produce similar pellets of fish bones and scales. These are of value to zoologists studying the feeding habits of such birds.

Below: Peregrine falcons (Falco peregrinus) *are adept aerial hunters, with pigeons – including homing pigeons – featuring prominently in their diet. These birds of prey display not just speed, but also superb manoeuvrability in flight, when pursuing their quarry.*

Birds of prey

Some avian predators feed mainly on other birds, such as the sparrowhawk (*Accipiter nisus*) – which is so-called because of its preference for hunting house sparrows (*Passer domesticus*). Another avian hunter, the peregrine falcon (*Falco peregrinus*), is among the most agile of all hunting birds. Strength is a feature of some species that prey on mammals, such as the golden eagle (*Aquila chrysaetos*), which can lift young lambs in its powerful talons, but often feeds on carrion. Yet other birds of prey target different groups of vertebrates,

Above: Vision is the main sense that allows most birds of prey, such as golden eagles (Aquila chrysaetos), *to target their victims. These eagles have keen sight.*

including fish and reptiles, while a great many species hunt insects and other invertebrates.

Hunting techniques

Many predatory birds hunt during the day, but not all, with most owls preferring to seek their prey at night. Mice and other creatures that are caught by owls are killed and eaten immediately. In contrast, shrikes (Laniidae) have a grisly reputation because they kill more prey than they can eat at once. They store the surplus as a so-called larder, impaling invertebrates such as grasshoppers, and sometimes even small vertebrates, on to sharp vegetation. Having secured their prey in this manner, they will then return to feed on them later. Caching, as this behaviour is known, is especially common during the breeding period, and presumably developed as a way of ensuring that the shrikes have sufficient food to rear their young.

Some birds have evolved particular ways of overcoming prey in certain localities. In parts of Egypt, for example, eagles have learnt to prey on

Above: Like other cormorants, the white-necked cormorant (Phalacrocorax carbo) *brings fish that it catches underwater up to the surface before swallowing them.*

Cormorants (Phalacrocoracidae) dive down after fish, and can remain submerged for some time. Kingfishers (*Alcedo atthis*) have sharp eyesight. Having detected the presence of a fish from the air, they dive into the water, seizing their quarry in their pointed bill and then re-emerging immediately. They then kill the fish by battering it against their perch. The speed at which the kingfisher dives provides the momentum to break through the surface, and it closes its wings once submerged to reduce resistance.

Aquatic predators always try to swallow their prey such as fish head-first. That way, gills and scales do not get stuck in their throat. On land, predatory birds that hunt victims such as rodents employ a similar technique so they do not choke on fur and tails.

Scavengers

Vultures are the best-known of all scavengers. They can home in on carcasses from a great distance away, and so have become regarded as harbingers of death. Lammergeiers (*Gypaetus barbatus*) have developed a technique that allows them to feed on bones that their relatives cannot break open. They smash the bones into pieces by dropping them from a great height. It is a skill that they learn to perfect by choosing the right terrain on which to drop the bones.

The small Egyptian vulture (*Neophron percnopterus*) survives by using its small size, which is no match

Above: Precise judgement allows a kingfisher (Alcedo atthis) *to strike with deadly accuracy from a perch. These birds frequent stretches of clear water for this reason.*

at the site of a kill, to advantage: it can become airborne soon after dawn – before the thermal air currents needed by its larger relatives have been created – and seek out overnight casualities. In some parts of Africa, these vultures smash tough ostrich eggs by repeatedly throwing stones at them.

Birds other than vultures also scavenge on occasion rather than hunting. Road kills of birds and other animals offer rich pickings for a host of such species, ranging from corvids such as crows and magpies to road-runners (*Geococcyx californianus*).

Below: Griffon vultures (Gyps fulvus) *and similar scavengers usually have bald heads, because any plumage here would quickly become matted with blood.*

tortoises by seizing the unfortunate reptiles in their talons, and then dropping them on to rocky ground from the air to split open their shells.

Not all birds of prey are aerial predators. Species such as secretary birds (*Sagittarius serpentarius*), which range widely across Africa in grassland areas, prefer to seek their victims on the ground. Secretary birds have developed long, strong legs and yet have surprisingly small feet. Snakes feature prominently in the diet of these birds, which raise their wings when confronting one of the reptiles. This has the effect of breaking up the bird's outline, making it harder for the snake to strike. Meanwhile the bird uses its feet to stun the reptile by jumping up and down on it, before killing it with a stab of its sharp bill.

Aquatic predators

The osprey (*Pandion haliaetus*) is an unusual bird of prey that literally scoops up large fish swimming close to the water's surface while in flight. Other birds actually enter the water in search of their prey. They may not have sharp talons, but many have powerful bills that enable them to grab slippery fish without difficulty.

Pelicans are equipped with a large, capacious pouch beneath the lower part of their bill, which they use like a net to trawl the water for fish.

DISPLAY AND PAIRING

Birds' breeding habits vary greatly. Some birds pair up only fleetingly, while others do so for the whole breeding season, and some species pair for life. For many young cock birds, the priority is to gain a territory as the first step in attracting a partner. Birds use both plumage and their songs to attract a mate.

A number of factors trigger the onset of the breeding period. In temperate areas, as the days start to lengthen in spring, the increase in daylight is detected by the pineal gland in the bird's brain, which starts a complex series of hormonal changes in the body. Most birds form a bond with a single partner during the breeding season, which is often preceded by an elaborate display by the cock bird.

Bird song

Many cock birds announce their presence by their song, which both attracts would-be mates and establishes a claim to a territory. Once pairing has occurred, the male may cease singing, but in some cases he starts to perform a duet with the hen, with each bird singing in turn.

Singing obviously serves to keep members of the pair in touch with each other. In species such as Central and

Above: A male ruff (Philomachus pugnax) at a lek, where males compete with each other in displays to attract female partners. Ruffs do not form lasting pair bonds, so the hens nest on their own after mating has occurred.

South American wood quails (*Odontophorus*), the pair co-ordinate their songs so precisely that although the cock bird may sing the first few notes, and then the hen, it sounds as if the song is being sung by just one bird. Other birds may sing in unison. In African gonoleks (*Laniarius*), it may even be possible to tell the length of time that the pair have been together by the degree of harmony in their particular songs.

Studies have revealed that young males birds start warbling quite quietly, and then sing more loudly as they mature. Finally, when their song pattern becomes fixed, it remains constant throughout the bird's life.

It is obviously possible to identify different species by differences in their song patterns. However, there are sometimes marked variations between the songs of individuals of the same species that live in different places. Local dialects have been identified in various parts of a species' distribution, as in the case of grey parrots (*Psittacus erithacus*) from different parts of Africa. In addition, as far as some songbirds are concerned, recent studies

Below: An adult cock Fischer's whydah (Vidua fischeri) in breeding condition is easily distinguished from the rather plain-coloured hen by its magnificent plumage. For the remainder of the year, however, it is virtually impossible to distinguish between the sexes by sight. Whydahs occur exclusively in Africa.

Below: Male masked weavers (Ploceus) build nests as part of their displays to attract the females. The techniques involved in nest-building are extremely complex and can be mastered only with practice. Hens are likely to choose older males as partners because they have superior nest-building skills.

Above: Mute swans (Cygnus olor) *are one of the species that pair for life. They become highly territorial when breeding, but outside the nesting period they often form flocks on large stretches of water. In spite of their common name, they can vocalize to a limited extent, by hissing and even grunting.*

have shown that over the course of several generations, the pattern of song can alter markedly.

Birds produce their sounds – even those species capable of mimicking human speech – without the benefit of a larynx and vocal cords like humans. The song is created in a voice organ called the syrinx, which is located in the bird's throat, at the bottom of the windpipe, or trachea.

The structure of the syrinx is very variable, being at its most highly developed in songbirds, which possess as many as nine pairs of separate muscles to control the vocal output. As in the human larynx, it is the flow of air through the syrinx that enables the membranes here to vibrate, creating sound. An organ called the interclavicular air sac also plays an important role, and birds cannot sing without it. The depth of song is not always proportional to size. The small Cetti's warbler (*Cettia cetti*) of Great Britain will emit an explosion of clear, penetrating notes over a period of a few seconds, which ceases as abruptly as it began. When breeding, males will even sing at night to attract hens.

Breeding behaviour

Many birds rely on their breeding finery to attract their mates. Some groups assemble in communal display areas known as leks, where hens witness the males' displays and select a mate. A number of different species, ranging from game birds to birds of paradise (Paradisaeidae), establish leks. Other species use a combination of factors to attract a mate. Male weaver birds (Ploceidae), for example, moult at the onset of the breeding season to display brightly-coloured plumage, which is intended to lure the female bird to their elaborate nest. These complex constructions are made from densely packed grass and twigs, and

may even boast a long and complex entrance tunnel. The successful pairing of the weavers will depend finally on the female's approval of the nest. Hens often assent to breed with older cocks, whose nest-building abilities show more sophistication than those of the younger birds.

Pair bonding

Many male and female birds form no lasting relationship, although the pair bond may be strong during the nesting period. It is usually only in potentially long-lived species, such as the larger parrots (Psittacidae) and hornbills (Bucorvidae), or waterfowl such as swans (Anatidae), that a lifelong pair bond is formed.

Pair bonding in long-lived species has certain advantages. The young of such birds are slow to mature, and are often unlikely to nest for five years or more. By remaining for a time in a family group, and sheltering the developing birds until they are strong enough to fend for themselves, adults can improve the survival prospects of their young.

Below: The dance of sandhill cranes (Grus canadensis) *is one of the most spectacular sights in the avian world, reinforcing the lifelong pair bond in this species. Dancing starts with the trumpeting calls of the birds as they stand side-by-side. Both sexes then start to leap into the air and display, raising their wings and tail feathers. Sometimes the birds even pick up sticks and toss them into the air.*

NESTING AND EGG-LAYING

All birds reproduce by laying eggs, which are covered with a hard, calcareous shell. The number of eggs laid at a time – known as the clutch size – varies significantly between species, as does egg coloration. Nesting habits also vary, with some birds constructing very elaborate nests.

The coloration and markings of a bird's eggs are directly linked to the nesting site. Birds that usually breed in hollow trees produce white eggs, because these are normally hidden from predators and so do not need to be camouflaged. The pale coloration may also help the adult birds to locate the eggs as they return to the nest, thus lessening the chances of damaging them. Birds that build more open, cup-shaped nests tend to lay coloured eggs, often with a mottled pattern – this acts as a useful camouflage, making them less obvious to potential nest thieves.

Nesting holes

Many birds use tree holes for nesting. Woodpeckers (Picidae) are particularly well equipped to create nesting chambers, using their powerful bills to enlarge holes in dead trees. The diameter of the entry hole thus created

Below: Ostriches lay the largest eggs in the world, which can weigh up to 1.5kg (3.3lb). In comparison, a chicken's egg, shown in front of the ostrich egg, looks tiny. The egg nearest to the viewer is a hummingbird egg. These tiny birds lay the smallest eggs in the avian world, weighing only about 0.35g (0.01oz).

Above: African bee-eaters (Merops species) nest colonially, which can make them conspicuous. They will seek to make these breeding sites inaccessible, however, typically burrowing into sandy cliffs.

is just wide enough to allow the birds to enter easily, which helps to prevent the nest being robbed. Hornbills (Bucorvidae) go one stage further – the cock bird walls the hen up inside the nest. He plasters the hole over with mud, leaving just a small gap through which he can feed the female. The barrier helps to protect the nest from attacks by snakes and lizards. The female remains entombed inside until her young are well grown. At this stage she breaks out and then helps her mate to rear the chicks, having walled them back up again.

Nest-building

Some birds return to the same nest site each year, but many birds simply abandon their old nest and build another. This may seem a waste of effort, but it actually helps to protect the birds from parasites such as blood-sucking mites, which can otherwise multiply in the confines of the nest. Most birds construct their nests from vegetation, depending on which

The reproductive systems

The cock bird has two testes located within his body. Spermatozoa pass down the vas deferens, into the cloaca and then out of the body. Insemination occurs when the vent areas of the male and female bird are in direct contact during mating. Cock birds do not have a penis for penetration, although certain groups, such as waterfowl, may have a primitive organ that is used to assist in the transference of semen in a similar way.

Normally only the left ovary and oviduct of the hen bird are functional. Eggs pass down through the reproductive tract from the ovary. Spermatozoa swim up the hen's reproductive tract, and fertilize the ova at an early stage in the process. Generally, only one mating is required to fertilize a clutch of eggs. Spermatozoa may sometimes remain viable in the hen's body for up to three weeks following mating.

1 Kidneys
2 Testes
3 Vas deferens
4 Cloaca

5 Ova
6 Infundibulum

7 Magnum
8 Isthmus
9 Egg with shell contained in the hen's reproductive tract
10 Cloaca

Male

Female

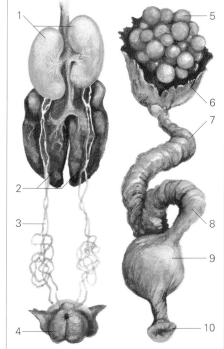

materials are locally available. In coastal areas, some seabirds use pieces of seaweed to build theirs. Artificial materials such as plastic wrappers or polystyrene may be used by some birds.

Nest styles

Different types of birds build nests of various shapes and sizes, which are characteristic of their species. Groups such as finches build nests in the form of an open cup, often concealed in vegetation. Most pigeons and doves construct a loose platform of twigs. Swallows are among the birds that use mud to construct their nests. They scoop muddy water up from the surface of a pond or puddle, mould it into shape on a suitable wall, and then allow it to dry and harden like cement.

The simplest nests are composed of little more than a pad of material, resting in the fork of a tree or on a building. The effort entailed in nest construction may reflect how often the birds are likely to nest. The platforms of pigeons and doves can disintegrate quite easily, resulting in the loss of eggs or chicks. However, if disaster does befall the nest, the pair will often breed again within a few weeks. At the other end of the scale, albatrosses expend considerable effort on nesting, because if failure occurs, the pair may not breed again for two years or so.

Cup-shaped nests are more elaborate than platform nests, being usually made by weaving grasses and twigs together. The inside is often lined with soft feathers. The raised sides of the cup nest lessen the likelihood of losing eggs and chicks, and also offer greater security to the adults during incubation. The hollow in the nest's centre is created by the birds compressing the material here before egg-laying begins.

Suspended nests enclosed by a domed roof offer even greater security. They are less accessible to predators because of their design and also their position, often hanging from slender branches. Some waxbills (*Estrilda*) build a particularly elaborate nest, comprising two chambers. There is an obvious upper opening, which is

Above: A pair of fulmars (Fulmarus glacialis) at their nest. Choosing a location close to the sea means they can obtain food easily, and the cliffs themselves afford some shelter.

always empty, suggesting to would-be predators that the nest is unoccupied. The birds occupy the chamber beneath, which has a separate opening.

Nest protection

Some birds rely on the safety of numbers to deter would-be predators, building vast communal nests that are occupied by successive generations and added to regularly. The so-called social weavers (*Philetairus socius*) of the African Kalahari region tend to breed in this way. A single nest, which is constructed by both sexes, may house up to 400 birds, and contain as many as 100 entrances. The nests themselves resemble an enormous thatched mass

of straw and other vegetation – often likened to a suspended haystack – and are usually built in native trees or even around manmade structures such as telegraph poles, which they tend to engulf entirely. Most incredibly of all, each entrance to the nest is reinforced with sharp grass straws, pointing down like spears, to ward off predators. The interior of the nest contains a network of cosy chambers, lined with feathers, which are used not only for breeding purposes, but also as a cool retreat from soaring daytime temperatures.

Other birds have evolved different methods not only of protecting their nests, but also of minimizing the time in which they spend incubating their eggs. Various parrots, such as the red-faced lovebirds (*Agapornis pullaria*) of Africa, lay their eggs in termite mounds. The insects tolerate this intrusion, while the heat of the mound keeps the eggs warm.

Birds that nest on the ground, such as the stone curlew (*Burhinus oedicnemus*), are especially vulnerable to predators and rely heavily on their fairly drab plumage as camouflage. Skylarks (*Alauda arvensis*) have another means of protecting their nest site – they hold one wing down and pretend to be injured to draw a predator away.

Below: Most eggs have a generally rounded shape, but seabirds such as guillemots (Uria aalge) breeding on rocky outcrops lay eggs that are more pointed. This shape helps to prevent the eggs from rolling over the cliff.

HATCHING AND REARING CHICKS

Birds are vulnerable to predators when breeding, especially when they have young in the nest. The chicks must be fed frequently, necessitating regular trips to and from the nest, which makes it conspicuous. The calls of the young birds represent a further danger, so the breeding period is often short.

Most birds incubate their eggs to keep them sufficiently warm for the chicks to develop inside. Larger eggs are less prone to chilling during incubation than small eggs, because of their bigger volume. In the early stages of the incubation period, when the nest may be left uncovered while the adult birds are foraging for food, eggs can withstand a lower temperature. Temperature differences also account for the fact that, at similar altitudes, incubation periods tend to be slightly longer in temperate areas than in tropical regions.

The eggshell may appear to be a solid barrier but in fact contains many pores, which are vital to the chick's well-being. These tiny holes allow water vapour and carbon dioxide to escape from the egg, and oxygen to enter it to reach the embryo.

Incubation

The incubation period often does not start until more than one egg has been laid, and sometimes not until the entire clutch has been completed. The interval between the laying of one egg and the next varies – finches lay every

Below: A fertile chicken's egg, showing the development of the embryo through to hatching. 1. The fertilized egg cell divides to form a ball of cells that gradually develops into an embryo. 2. The embryo develops, nourished by the yolk sac. 3. The air space at the rounded end of the egg enlarges as water evaporates. 4. The chick is almost fully developed and ready to hatch. 5. The chick cuts its way out, and its feathers dry off.

day, whereas gannets may lay only one egg every six days. If incubation does not start until egg-laying has finished, the chicks will all be of a similar size when they hatch, which increases their overall chances of survival.

The cock and hen may share incubation duties, as in the case of most pigeons and doves, or just one member of the pair may incubate. While this is usually the hen, there are exceptions. With ostriches (*Struthio*

Above: Breeding in one of the coldest places on Earth means that emperor penguins (Aptenodytes forsteri) can lay only a single egg, which they incubate on top of their feet, where special blood vessels help to warm it. After hatching, the chick is carried here too.

camelus) and other large flightless birds, it is the male who incubates the eggs, and cares for the resulting chicks. Anis (*Crotophaga*) breed communally, and all members of the group share the task of incubation.

1   2   3   4   5

Nest parasites

Nest parasitism is common in many species of cuckoo, such as the European cuckoo (*Cuculus canorus*). The males do not establish breeding territories, but mate with females at random. The females lay a single egg in the nests of host species such as reed warblers (*Acrocephalus scirpaceus*). The rapid development of the cuckoo's egg is vital so that the chick hatches first, and can then throw the other eggs or chicks out of the nest. In this way, it monopolizes the food supply brought by its foster parents. Any other chicks that do survive this initial stage die later, as they lose out in competition for food with their gigantic nest mate.

Below: Foster parents such as this reed warbler continue to feed the young cuckoo even when the imposter dwarfs them in size.

Hatching

Incubation periods vary among species, ranging from as few as 11 days in the case of some sparrows (*Spizella*), to over 80 days in some albatrosses (Diomedeidae). Before hatching, the chick uses the egg tooth on the tip of its upper bill to cut through the inner membrane into the air space at the blunt end of the shell, which forms as water evaporates from the egg. The chick starts to breathe atmospheric air for the first time. About 48 hours later, it breaks through the shell to emerge from the egg.

Chicks hatch out at various stages of development, and are accordingly able to leave the nest sooner or later.

Species that remain in the nest for some time after hatching, including parrots (Psittaciformes) and finches (Fringillidae), hatch in a blind and helpless state and are entirely dependent on their parents at first. Birds in this group are known as nidicolous. If not closely brooded, they are likely to become fatally chilled. In contrast, species that leave the nest soon after hatching, known as nidifugous, emerge from the egg and are able to move around on their own at this stage. They can also see, and feed themselves, almost immediately. The offspring of many game birds such as pheasants as well as waterfowl and waders are nidifugous, which gives them a better chance of survival, as they can run to escape from predators. Young waterfowl cannot take safely to the water at first, however, because they lack the oil from the preen gland above the base of the tail to water-proof their feathers.

Rearing and fledging

Many adult birds offer food to their offspring, even some nidifugous species. This can be a particularly demanding period, especially for small birds that have relatively large broods. Great tits (*Parus major*), for example, must supply their offspring with huge quantities of insects. They typically feed their chicks up to 60 times an hour, as well as keeping the nest clean.

Young birds usually leave the nest from about 12 to 30 days after hatching. However, some species develop much more slowly. Albatross chicks are particularly slow developers, spending up to eight and a half months in the nest.

When they first leave the nest, many young birds are unable to fly, simply because their flight feathers are not fully functional. If these feathers are not fully unfurled from the protective sheaths in which they emerged, they cannot function effectively. The strength of the wing muscles also needs to be built up, so it is not uncommon for young birds to rest on the sides of the nest, flapping their wings occasionally, before finally taking to the air for the first time. Chicks that

Above: Blue tits (Parus caeruleus) *are typical of many birds that leave the nest before they are able to fly effectively. The young remain hidden in vegetation and are fed by their parents in these critical early days after leaving the nest.*

are unable to fly immediately on fledging remain reliant on the adults, especially the cock, for food until they become fully independent.

For some young seabirds, fledging is a particularly hazardous process. From their cliff-ledge nests, they may simply flop down onto the water, where they are at risk from drowning until they master swimming skills. If they get swept out to sea, they may be caught by predators such as killer whales.

Below: The broad and often colourful gape of chicks allows parent birds such as this blackcap warbler (Sylvia atricapilla) *to feed their offspring quickly and efficiently. Weak chicks that are unable to raise their heads and gape at the approach of a parent will quickly die from starvation.*

SURVIVAL

The numbers of a particular species of bird can vary significantly over time, affected by factors such as the availability of food, climate, disease and hunting. When the reproductive rate of a species falls below its annual mortality rate, it is in decline, but this does not mean it will inevitably become extinct.

For many birds, life is short and hazardous. Quite apart from the risk of predation, birds can face a whole range of other dangers, from starvation and disease through to inadvertent interference or persecution by humans. The reproductive rate is higher and age of maturity is lower in species that have particularly hazardous lifestyles, such as blue tits (*Parus caeruleus*). These species often breed twice or more each year in rapid succession.

Rising and falling numbers

Some birds will travel long distances from their native habitat when living conditions become unfavourable. Pallas's sandgrouse (*Syrrhaptes paradoxus*), for instance, a species normally found in central and eastern parts of Asia, has occasionally invaded the more temperate habitats of western Europe to breed. Large-scale irruptions of this type were recorded in 1863, 1868 and 1908, involving thousands of birds, and sightings were made from

Below: These lesser flamingos (Phoenicopterus minor) live together in large groups, as they require a very specific habitat for dietary needs and breeding. Group living brings advantages in that it is easier to find a mate, and the presence of so many eyes will alert the birds to dangers more quickly than with pairs or lone birds.

the Faeroe Islands in the far North Atlantic, southwards to Spain, with numerous identifications in the British Isles. Despite these often protracted relocations to ensure survival, the range of the grouse has never extended permanently into Europe.

Similar fluctuations affect other bird colonies when food runs into short supply. Snowy owls (*Nyctea scandiaca*) have a circumpolar range throughout northern Europe and North America, and the diet of the latter population depends heavily on the availability of lemmings to eat. When a combination of environmental factors causes the numbers of these small mammals to

Above: Some parents, like these scarlet-chested sunbirds (Nectarinia senegalensis), keep watch over their young until the juveniles have grown relatively large in size.

plummet, the predatory owls are forced to spread out over a much wider area in search of food, and their breeding success plummets accordingly. As the lemming population recovers, so too will the number of snowy owls gradually rise again. This is a good example of how the interdependence of species sharing a habitat prompts cyclical change in, and subsequent control of, their numbers.

Group living

Safety in numbers is a major benefit of group living, as it can bring increased protection to birds both in the air and on the ground. For example, the way in which flocks manage to co-ordinate their flight, by weaving, dipping and rising together as a group, makes it far more difficult for an aerial predator to focus on an individual. Coloration can also disguise the number of individuals within a flock, and it serves to protect more vulnerable lone birds too. The mottled colouring on the head and upperparts of many shore and game birds, for instance, breaks up their outline so that, while on the ground, they merge more effectively against the land and are less conspicuous to birds of prey circling above. On sensing danger overhead, these advantageously coloured birds will often freeze into position and hold very still until the threat has passed, taking care not to betray their presence by a single movement – a far better guarantee of survival than taking flight or scurrying to find shelter.

Effects of humans
It is generally assumed that human interference in the landscape is likely to have harmful effects on avian populations. However, this is not always the case. The expansion of agriculture in various parts of West Africa, especially of crops such as millet, has resulted in the availability of more concentrated supplies of food. This, in turn, has enabled many smaller seed-eating birds such as the golden song sparrow (*Passer luteus*) to increase so rapidly in such locations that their numbers have reached plague proportions. Subsequent attempts to control the level of this increase have, in some cases, been less than humane – there are even reports of napalm gas being used against roosting sites. Other birds have, however, been boosted by direct human intervention, such as the common starling (*Sturnus vulgaris*). These birds have spread across North America, following their introduction from Europe in the late 1800s.

Similarly, the common pheasant (*Phasianus colchicus*), a native of Asia, is now found across much of Europe, thanks to human interest in these game birds, which are bred in large numbers for sport shooting. Many more survive than would otherwise be the case, thanks to the attention of gamekeepers who not only provide food, but also help to curb possible predators in areas where the birds are released.

Slow breeders
Birds that reproduce slowly, such as albatrosses (Diomedeidae) and sandhill cranes (*Grus canadensis*), are likely to be highly vulnerable to any changes in their surroundings, whether caused by

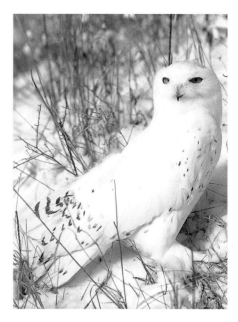

Above: Snowy owls (Nyctea scandiaca) *are often seen near coasts outside the breeding season. They are opportunistic hunters, even catching fish on occasion.*

human interference, climate change, disease, or other factors. Great concern has recently been focused on albatross numbers, which are declining worldwide. Many of these birds have been caught and drowned in fishing nets in recent years. Albatrosses are normally very long-lived and breed very slowly. Any sudden decline in their population is therefore likely to have devastating consequences that cannot easily be reversed.

Below: The black-shouldered kite (Elanus caeruleus), *seen here with its young, is an adaptable and wide-ranging bird of prey, with the ability to breed not just in Africa, but in parts of Europe and Southern Asia too.*

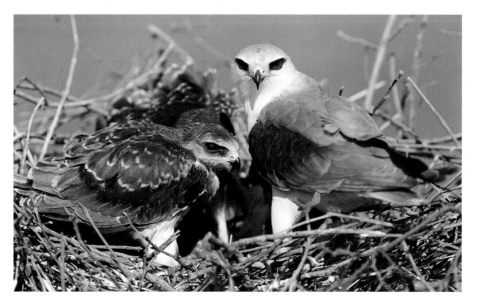

MIGRATION

Some birds live in a particular place all year round, but many are only temporary visitors. Typically, species fly north into temperate latitudes in spring, and return south at the end of summer. They have a wide distribution, but are seen only in specific parts of their range at certain times of the year.

Many species of birds – known as "migrants" – regularly undertake seasonal movements on specific routes. Migrations are different from so-called irruptions, when flocks suddenly move to an area where conditions are more favourable. Birds migrate to seek shelter from the elements, to find safe areas to rear their young and, in particular, to seek places where food is plentiful. Birds such as waxwings (Bombycillidae) irrupt to a new location to find food when supplies become scarce in their habitat, but such journeys are less frequent and are irregular. The instinct to migrate dates

Right: Various routes between Europe and Africa are chosen by migrants such as warblers, swallows, birds of prey and storks. Some species native to Asia also cross these pathways from the east. Crossings are not usually direct, if this would involve a potentially hazardous ocean journey. This is why birds from Iceland, for example, usually fly down across the British Isles to reach Africa, rather than veering west over the Atlantic. Even when crossing smaller bodies of water such as the Mediterranean, birds will instinctively follow routes where the land masses are close together, such as via the Iberian peninsula.

Below: Some southern European populations of Canada geese (Branta canadensis) are now losing their migratory instincts, as the winters here are less harsh and food is quite plentiful.

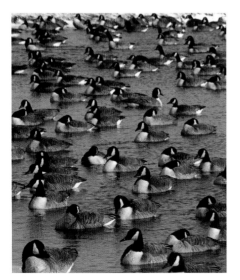

back millions of years, to a period when the seasons were often much more extreme, which meant that it was difficult to obtain food in a location throughout the year. This forced birds to move in search of food. Even today, the majority of migratory species live within the world's temperate zones, particularly the Northern Hemisphere, where seasonal change is pronounced.

Migratory routes

The routes that the birds follow on their journeys are often well defined. Land birds try to avoid flying over large stretches of water, preferring instead to follow coastal routes and crossing the sea at the shortest point. For instance, many birds migrating from Europe to Africa prefer to fly over the Straits of Gibraltar. Frequently

Banding birds

Much of what we know about migration and the lifespan of birds comes from banding studies carried out by ornithologists. Bands placed on the birds' legs allow experts to track their movements when the ringed birds are recovered again. The rings are made of lightweight aluminium, and have details of the banding organization and when banding was carried out. Unfortunately, only a very small proportion of ringed birds are ever recovered, so the data gathered is incomplete, but now other methods of tracking, such as radar, are also used to follow the routes taken by flocks of birds, which supplements the information from banding studies.

Below: A mute swan (Cygnus olor) *wearing a band. Coloured bands can help to identify individual birds from some distance away.*

birds fly at much greater altitudes when migrating. Cranes (Gruidae) have been recorded flying at 5,000m (16,400ft) when crossing the mountainous areas in France, and geese (*Anser*) have been observed crossing the Himalayas at altitudes of more than 9,000m (29,500ft). Even if the migratory routes are known, it is often difficult to spot migrating birds because they fly so high.

Speed and distance

Migrating birds also fly at greater speeds than usual, which helps to make their journey time as short as possible. The difference can be significant – migrating swallows (*Hirundo rustica*) travel at speeds between 3 and 14km/h (1.8–8.7mph) faster than usual, and are assisted by the greater altitude, where the air is thinner and resistance is less.

Some birds travel huge distances on migration. Arctic terns (*Sterna paradisea*), for example, cover distances of more than 15,000km (9,300 miles) in total, as they shuttle between the Arctic and Antarctic. They fly an average distance of 160km (100 miles) every day. Size does not preclude birds from migrating long distances, either. The tiny ruby-throated hummingbird (*Archilochus colubris*) flies over the Gulf of Mexico from the eastern USA every year, a distance of more than 800km (500 miles).

Preparing for migration

The migratory habits of birds have long been the subject of scientific curiosity. As late as the 1800s, it was thought that swallows hibernated in the bottom of ponds because they were seen skimming over the pond surface in groups before disappearing until the following spring. Now we know that they were probably feeding on insects to build up energy supplies for their long journey ahead.

Even today, the precise mechanisms involved in migratory behaviour are not fully understood. We do know that birds feed up before setting out on migration, and that various hormonal changes enable them to store more fat

Above: Many birds, including this bluethroat (Luscinta suecica), *set out on migration after moulting. Damaged plumage can make the task of flying harder.*

in their bodies to sustain them on their journey. Feeding opportunities are likely to be more limited than usual when birds are migrating, while their energy requirements are, of course, higher. In addition, birds usually moult just before migrating, so that their plumage is in the best condition to withstand the inevitable buffeting that lies ahead.

Navigation

Birds use both learned and visual cues to orientate themselves when migrating. Young birds of many species, such as swans, learn the route by flying in the company of their elders. However, some young birds set out on their own and reach their destinations successfully without the benefit of experienced companions, navigating by instinct alone. Birds such as swifts (Apopidae) fly mainly during daytime, whereas others, including ducks (Anatidae), migrate at night. Many birds fly direct to their destination, but some may detour and break their journey to obtain food and water before setting out again.

Experiments have shown that birds orientate themselves using the position of the sun and stars, as well as by following familiar landmarks. They also use the Earth's magnetic field to find their position, and thus do not get lost in cloudy or foggy weather, when the sky is obscured. The way in which these various factors come together, however, is not yet fully understood.

BEHAVIOUR

Bird behaviour, or avian ethology as it is known, is a very broad field. Some patterns of behaviour are common to all birds, whereas other actions are very specific, just to a single species or even to an individual population. Interpreting behaviour is easier in some cases than in others.

All bird behaviour essentially relates to various aspects of survival, such as avoiding predators, feeding, finding a mate and breeding successfully. Some behaviour patterns are instinctive, while others develop in certain populations of birds in response to particular conditions. Thus the way in which birds behave is partly influenced by their environment as well as being largely instinctual.

Age also plays a part in determining behaviour, since younger birds often behave in a very different way to the

Above: The posture a bird adopts while sunbathing can appear to indicate distress, as is the case with this Eurasian blackbird (Turdus merula), *which is resting with its bill open and wings outstretched.*

adults. Some forms of bird behaviour are relatively easy to interpret, while others are a great deal more difficult to explain.

Garden birds
One of the first studies documenting birds' ability to adapt their behaviour in response to changes in their environment involved blue tits (*Parus caeruleus*) in Britain. The study showed that certain individuals learned to use their bills to tap through the shiny metallic foil covers on milk bottles to reach the milk. Other blue tits followed their example, and in certain areas householders with milk deliveries had to protect their bottle tops from the birds.

The way in which birds have learned to use various types of garden feeders also demonstrates their ability to modify their existing behaviour in response to new conditions when it benefits them. A number of new feeders on the market designed to thwart squirrels from stealing the food

exploit birds' ability to adapt in this way. The birds have to squeeze through a small gap to reach the food, just as they might enter the nest. Once one bird has been bold enough to enter in this fashion, others observe and soon follow suit.

Preening
Although preening serves a variety of functions, the most important aspect is keeping the feathers in good condition. It helps to dislodge parasites and removes loose feathers, particularly during moulting. It also ensures that the plumage is kept waterproof by spreading oil from the preen gland at the base of the tail.

Preening can be a social activity too. It may be carried out by pairs of males and females during the breeding season, or among a family group.

Aggression
Birds can be surprisingly aggressive towards each other, even to the point of sometimes inflicting fatal injuries. Usually, however, only a few feathers are shed before the weaker individual backs away, without sustaining serious injury. Conflicts of this type can break out over feeding sites or territorial disputes. The risk of aggressive outbreaks is greatest at the start of the breeding season, when the territorial instincts of cock birds are most aroused. Size is no indicator of the potential level of aggression, since some of the smallest birds, such as sunbirds (Nectarinidae), can be ferociously aggressive towards each other.

Below: A dispute breaks out between a pair of European nutcrackers (Nucifraga caryocatactes). *Birds often fight with their wings outstretched, as they seek to batter their opponent into submission.*

This behaviour is seen in a variety of birds, ranging from parrots to finches. Some parrots perform mutual preening throughout the year, which reinforces the pair bond. In some species of psittaculid parakeets, however, such as the African ring-necked (*Psittacula krameri*), the dominant hen allows her mate to preen her only when she is in breeding condition, and therefore preening in this instance may be seen as a prelude to mating.

Bathing

Preening is not the only way in which birds keep their plumage in good condition. Birds often bathe to remove dirt and debris from their plumage. Small birds wet their feathers by lying on a damp leaf during a shower of rain, in an activity known as leaf-bathing. Other birds immerse themselves in a pool of water, splashing around and ruffling their feathers.

Some birds, especially those found in drier areas of the world, prefer to dust-bathe, lying down in a dusty hollow known as a scrape and using fine earth thrown up by their wings to absorb excess oil from their plumage. Then, by shaking themselves thoroughly, followed by a period of preening, the excess oil is removed.

Sunbathing

Sunbathing may be important in allowing birds to synthesize Vitamin D3 from the ultraviolet rays in sunlight, which is vital for a healthy skeleton. This process can be achieved only by light falling on the bird's skin, which explains why birds ruffle their plumage at this time. Some birds habitually stretch out while sunbathing, while others, such as many pigeons, prefer to rest with one wing

Right: The natural waterproofing present on the plumage ensures that birds do not become saturated when swimming or caught in a shower of rain. This would destroy the warm layer of air surrounding the body created by the down feathering, and leave them vulnerable to hypothermia. Nevertheless birds do need to dry their plumage, which is what this cormorant (Phalacrocorax carbo) is doing, with its wings outstretched.

raised, leaning over at a strange angle on the perch. Vasa parrots (*Coracopsis*), found on the island of Madagascar, frequently behave in this fashion – however, sunbathing is generally not common in this group of birds.

Maintaining health

Some people believe that when birds are ill, they eat particular plants that have medicinal properties, but this theory is very difficult to prove. One form of behaviour that does confer health benefits has been documented, however: it involves the use of ants. Instead of eating these insects, some birds occasionally rub them in among their feathers. This causes the ants to release formic acid, which acts as a potent insecticide, killing off lurking parasites such as mites and lice. Jays (*Garrulus glandarius*) and also starlings (Sturmidae) and Eurasian blackbirds (*Turdus merula*) are among the species that have been observed using insects in this way. Members of the crow family have also been seen perching on smoking chimney pots or above bonfires, ruffling their feathers and allowing the smoke to penetrate their plumage. The smoke is thought to kill off parasites in a process that confers the same benefits as anting.

Above: Birds such as the African yellow-billed oxpecker (Buphagus africanus) *form unusual associations with large mammals. These starlings frequently hitch a ride on the backs of animals such as rhinoceroses, as seen here, and buffaloes, where they are relatively safe from predators, and can feed on the animal's resident colony of ticks.*

Below: The Eurasian green woodpecker (Picus viridis) *uses its strong, pointed bill to pluck invertebrates from the ground.*

BIRDWATCHING

Thanks to their widespread distribution, birds can be seen in virtually any locality, even in the centre of cities. You don't need any special equipment to watch birds, but a pair of binoculars will help you to gain a better insight into avian behaviour, by allowing you to study birds at close range.

Birdwatching can be carried out almost anywhere around the world. Many people enjoy simply watching the birds that visit their garden. A greater variety of species can be seen if the birdwatcher ventures further afield, to local parks, woods or wetlands for example. Birdwatching holidays and sponsored birdwatching competitions offer opportunities to see an even greater variety of birds in different locations. Seasonal changes in bird populations mean that even if you visit the same area through the year, you will see new species at different times.

Above: At many major reserves where birds congregate, special permanent birdwatching hides have been set up to give visitors a good view without disturbing the birds themselves.

Getting a good view

Binoculars can be purchased from camera stores and similar outlets, but it is important to test them before deciding which model to buy, particularly as they vary quite significantly in price. When purchasing binoculars, you will need to consider not only the power of magnification, but also how closely the binoculars can be focused, particularly if you going to use them at home, where the bird table is likely to be relatively close.

Binoculars vary according to their power of magnification and the length of the objective lens in millimetres, with the lens modifying the image. The lens' length and magnification are given in the specifications: binoculars described as 8x45 multiply the image by 8 in comparison with how it would appear to the naked eye and have an objective lens of 45mm, which is important in determining the focus.

Two important considerations stem from the power of magnification. First, the depth of field is important, since it affects the area of the image that is in

---

Drawing birds for reference

1. Sketching birds is relatively straight-forward if you follow this procedure. Start by drawing an egg shape for the body, with a smaller egg above, which will become the head, and another to form the rump. A centre line through the head circle will form the basis for the bill. Now add circles and lines to indicate the position of the wings and tail. Add lines for the legs and then sketch in the feet and claws.

2. Use an indelible fine-line felt-tip pen to ink in the shape of the bird that you have drawn previously in pencil, avoiding the unwanted construction lines.

3. Coloured pencils will allow you to add more detail after you have rubbed out any unwanted pencil markings.

4. If you take a number of prepared head shapes with you into the field, you can fill in the detail quickly and easily, enabling you to identify birds later.

focus. The greater the magnification, the shallower the depth of field. A deep depth of field can be helpful, chiefly because it ensures that a larger proportion of the birds on view are in focus, which avoids the need to refocus constantly. If the depth of field is shallow, only the birds in the centre will be in focus. Second, the degree of magnification also affects the field of vision – the area that you can see through the binoculars. A wide field of vision will help you to locate birds more easily.

Buying binoculars

A number of other factors may be considered when buying binoculars.

• Weight is important. Consider buying a lightweight pair if you intend using binoculars for long periods. They should also feel balanced in the hands.

• For people with large hands, small binoculars may be hard to adjust and not very comfortable to hold. Pay attention to the focusing mechanism – it should be easy to operate.

• Try the eyecups of the binoculars to see how comfortable they feel. If you wear spectacles, it is important that the cups give you a full field of vision. Binoculars with adjustable eyecups are more suitable for spectacle-wearers.

• Is the design of good quality? It could be worthwhile paying extra for waterproofing. The better-quality

Below: A view of a hide. External camouflage, easy access and good viewing positions are essential features in the design of such units. Even so, it may take birds some time to accept the presence of a hide.

Above: A garden bird table will attract many species to feed, and if it is carefully sited, you should be able to see the birds easily, even from inside your home.

Right: Hanging cages are a compact type of food dispenser. They should be filled with special peanuts that are safe for birds. They may attract a wide variety of birds, including various tits, finches and even more unusual species, such as this great spotted woodpecker (Dendrocopos major).

models have their chambers filled with nitrogen gas to prevent any condensation developing.

• The design should be robust, with a solid protective casing.

Fieldscopes

Apart from binoculars, dedicated bird-watchers often use birding telescopes, called fieldscopes. These are ideal for use in hides as they can be mounted in various ways, using either a bench clamp fitting or a tripod. Fieldscopes are equipped with lenses similar to those in binoculars, but are more suited to long-term use, when you are watching a nest for example, as you do not have to keep holding the scope while waiting for a bird to return. Instead, attach the scope to a branch or bench and train it on the nest, then simply be patient until you see the bird return.

Making notes

When observing birds either in the garden or further afield, it is always useful to have a notebook handy to write down details and make sketches.

When sketching, proceed from a few quick pencil lines to a more finished portrait as time allows. Water-soluble pencils are helpful for colouring sketches, as the colours can be spread using water and a small paintbrush. If you spot a bird you cannot identify, jot down the details quickly in your notebook. Note the bird's colours and markings. Write down the length of the neck and legs, and note the bill shape. Assess the bird's size in relation to familiar species, and try to decide which family you think it belongs to. Your notes can then be compared with a field guide or other sources of information to identify the bird.

FIELDCRAFT

If you are seriously interested in birdwatching, you will need to develop fieldcraft skills. There is a significant difference between watching birds casually in a garden and tracking down particular species in remote areas, where preparation is important. Don't neglect your own safety in the wild.

Left: Hand-held binoculars or a viewing scope attached to a tripod can help you to study both common and rare species. Taking notes is useful, especially if you intend to write up details of your observations.

Research and careful preparation are vital to the success of any field trip. You should also select clothing and equipment suited to the particular place where you intend to study birds.

Clothing and equipment

Suitable clothing is vital to keep you warm and dry when birdwatching. Waterproof footwear will be needed when visiting wetlands, or after rain. Dull-coloured clothing will allow you to blend in with the landscape so you can approach the birds more closely. A camping mat can be useful if you intend spending time on the ground.

In addition to packing your binoculars, camera equipment and perhaps a viewing scope, you may also want to take a notebook or sketchpad. A field guide will help to identify birds, while a waterproof rucksack will protect all your belongings.

Preparation

It always helps to do your homework before setting out. Investigating the habits of the birds you hope to see will help you to decide on the best place to go, and the time of day when they are most likely to be seen. It may be useful to draw up a checklist highlighting key features of the species concerned in advance. You can then refer to these in the field. Studying a local map prior to your visit will help you to orientate yourself in new surroundings. Good preparation is especially important in areas where you are likely to be unfamiliar with the birds concerned.

Photography

In the past, birdwatchers relied on 35mm SLR cameras and telephoto lenses to record their sightings. Today, however, birders are increasingly using digital cameras. These work very well when combined via a connector to a viewing scope that magnifies the image, like a telephoto lens. Digital cameras have the further advantage that they do not require film, but store images in their memory. Unwanted pictures can simply be deleted, while the best images can be transferred to a computer and printed out. Although you will not run out of film, digital cameras do use a surprising amount of power, so remember to take spare

Below: Plumage details, such as the handsome markings of this nutcracker (Nucifraga caryocatactes), may be captured using a conventional camera with a telephoto lens, or using a digital camera or camcorder linked to a viewing scope.

batteries with you on field trips. Digital camcorders can also be linked with viewing scopes, and are more flexible than cameras. Not only does a camcorder enable you to record the bird's song – which can be significant, especially if there is any doubt about identification – but you can also obtain a sequence of still images, especially if you can see the bird from different angles. Flight patterns can be recorded in this way, which again can help with identification. Even in relatively dark surroundings, some camcorders will function well.

Using hides and cover

On recognized reserves, there are likely to be hides in the best localities for birdwatching. Hides allow you to observe birds at relatively close quarters, and also offer excellent opportunities to photograph or film birds in their natural habitat. Even so, patience is likely to be needed for successful birding, as there will be no guarantees that you will see the species you hope to spot.

In areas where no hide is available, take cover behind shrubs, tree trunks or raised banks, or even in a parked car. Birds are highly attuned to the

Below: There are now many organized trips taking keen birders to far-flung parts of the world, offering unique opportunities to see new birds in exotic localities.

Above: In some areas, there may not be any natural cover or hides available. To get very close, it is vital to dress inconspicuously so that you blend into the background, and try to keep as still as you possibly can. Birdwatching requires plenty of patience.

slightest hint of danger, such as humans approaching. In areas where no cover is available, stand, kneel or lie in a comfortable position and try to move as little as possible. When approaching birds, make sure your position is downwind, so the sounds of your approach don't frighten them away.

Seeking rarities

Birdwatching magazines can be useful in identifying sites where rarities have been spotted. For up-to-the-minute news, you will need to seek out either a regularly updated website or an information phone line giving details of the latest sightings. Birders with access to email can also receive bulletins listing where particular rarities have cropped up. These are most likely to be recorded after bad weather such as fierce storms which can blow migrant birds off-course.

Bear in mind that many people will be drawn to a place where an unusual species has been sighted, and it is important not to create a disturbance or to trespass on private land. Similarly, it is a criminal offence in some areas to disturb breeding birds. Always act in a responsible manner when birdwatching.

Getting the best results

• Plan well beforehand, including checking tide times if relevant. Tidal areas can be particularly hazardous where there is quicksand.
• Remember that bird populations may vary according to the time of year.
• Never neglect your own safety. Let someone else know where you are going, and when you intend to return.
• Check the weather forecast first, and take a mobile phone in case you get into difficulties.
• Take a local map and also a compass to guide you if you get lost. Allow enough time to locate and then observe the birds.

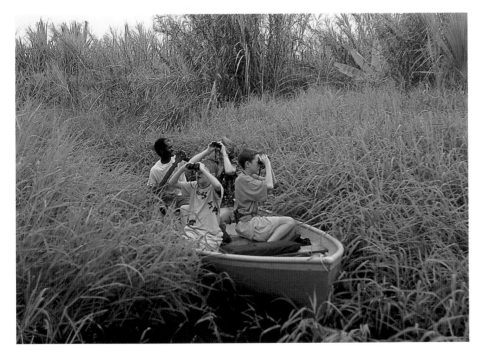

ZONES AND HABITATS

Birds have been exceedingly successful in colonizing the planet. Their warm-blooded nature and ability to fly have helped them to reach and then adapt to life in some of the world's most inaccessible places. They are found naturally on all continents, even successfully inhabiting Antarctica.

Zoologists divide the world into broad geographical zones, within which there are many different habitats. This approach reflects the movements of the Earth's landmasses through geological time, and so helps to show relationships between species occurring in various parts of the world today.

The Americas

In the distant past, North America was separated from its southern neighbour, and they had different origins. North America was originally attached to what is now Europe and later drifted westwards, while South America was once joined to a huge southern landmass that geologists call Gondwana, which included what is now the Indian subcontinent, Australia, Africa and Antarctica. South America split off at an earlier stage in

geological history than did North America – more than 100 million years ago – at a time when dinosaurs were in the ascendancy and the skies were occupied by flying reptiles called pterosaurs, rather than birds.

When birds began to evolve on this southern continent, they did so in isolation from the rest of the world. For this reason, the bird life that occurs today in this southern zone is known as neotropical, to distinguish it from that found in North America, which is known as nearctic. Later the avian populations of the Nearctic and Neotropical zones mingled somewhat by way of the Central American land bridge that was created when these two vast landmasses joined. However, unique forms still exist that are found only in South America, reflecting their isolated development in prehistory.

Above: This map shows how the different continents are believed to have formed and divided, giving rise to the familiar continents that we know today (see map below). These continental movements have had a direct effect on the distribution of avian life.

Above: The Indian subspecies of ring-necked parakeet (Psittacula krameri) *has succeeded in adapting to an urban existence in the suburbs of various European cities, including London and Amsterdam. Here the birds survive the winter mainly on bird-table offerings of seed put out for native birds.*

The Palaearctic

Europe has been separated from North America by the Atlantic Ocean for more than 50 million years, but the bird species of these now separate areas still show some evidence of their common past. In prehistory, Europe formed, and still forms, part of a much broader area known as the Palaearctic realm, which extends right across the northern continent from Iceland eastwards to Japan. Fossilized remains suggest that this region was the cradle of avian evolution, where the first members of the group probably originated more than 80 million years ago. Most zoologists believe that the oldest known bird, *Archaeopteryx*, was not in fact the first of the avian line, but as yet its immediate ancestors have not been discovered.

The distribution of avian species in the Northern Hemisphere has been affected in the more recent geological past by the spread and subsequent retreat of the ice sheets from the far north. Today, Europe and Asia experience a climate similar to that of the corresponding area of North America, ranging from arctic to subtropical according to latitude. The two regions even have some birds in common, especially in the far north, where certain species have a circumpolar distribution – they are found right around the polar region.

Africa, southern Asia and Australasia

As part of the great southern continent of Gondwana, Africa used to be attached to South America, but subsequently remained in contact with what is now the Indian subcontinent during the critical early phase in avian evolution approximately 60 million years ago. This distant history is reflected even today by the large number of avian species found south of what has become the Sahara Desert. This zone is now described as the Ethiopian realm, although it covers virtually all of Africa.

The Indian subcontinent became a separate landmass when Gondwana broke up. It ultimately drifted north, colliding and eventually joining with what is now the Asian landmass, and creating the Himalayan Mountains in the process. As in Africa, the broadly tropical climate and the landscape have altered little since then, which has meant that a number of the species that evolved here are found nowhere else in the world.

East and south of India lie the islands that comprise the Australasian realm, which includes Australia, New Guinea and New Zealand. These islands once formed part of the vast landmass of Gondwana, but later broke away and have been isolated from the rest of the world for millions of years. A diversity of bird species found nowhere else in the world can be seen here as a result.

Present distribution

Birds' current distribution throughout the world is affected by a number of different factors, as well as the history of their evolution. The ability to fly has allowed birds to become very widely distributed, as has their warm-blooded nature, which has meant that they are far less vulnerable to climatic factors than cold-blooded creatures. Lifestyle, and particularly the range of foods that are available, also play a part. When birdwatching, there are certain groups of birds that you are most likely to encounter in specific types of habitat as a result of all these factors. The major avian habitats of the world are as listed on the pages that follow.

Below: Common, or European, starlings (Sturnus vulgaris) *are now well established outside their natural range. They are now resident in the USA, having been introduced there in the 1800s. They have since spread out across North America, and can also be seen in other locations, including Australia.*

THE SEA

The world's oceans provide a very rich source of food for all birds able to exploit it. Fish and invertebrates such as squid and krill form the basis of the diet of seabirds, some of which range extensively across the world's oceans and are frequently sighted long distances from land.

The huge expanse of the oceans, and the difficulty of observing seabirds, means that relatively little is known about many species. This lack of knowledge was confirmed by the case of the Bermuda petrel (*Pterodroma cahow*). This species was believed to have become extinct during the 1600s, but, remarkably, a surviving population was rediscovered in 1951 after more than three hundred years. Seabirds survive out at sea with the help of special salt-excreting glands in

the nasal area (just above their bills) that allow them to drink seawater without getting dehydrated.

Breeding habits

Many seabirds are social by nature, forming huge breeding colonies on rocky outcrops by the sea. Indeed, one of the main factors restricting seabird populations can be the lack of nesting sites. By congregating in this way, the birds can maximize their reproductive success while reducing the attacks of predators on their numbers. Nest-raiders such as black-backed gulls (*Larus marinus*) may be unable to inflict major damage on a breeding colony if the birds are so densely packed that the raiders cannot land.

Feeding

The feeding habits of seabirds have a significant impact on their lifestyle. Albatrosses (Diomedeidae), for example, spend most of their lives flying above the oceans. Their large wingspan allows them to glide almost effortlessly for long periods, swooping down to take food from the surface or even catching flying fish above the waves, rather than entering the water. Other species, such as gannets (Sulidae), dive beneath the surface to feed.

Above: Birds have come to recognize trawlers as sources of fish, swooping down to feed on whatever is thrown overboard, and haunting shipping lanes. Fulmars (Fulmarus glacialis) and gannets (Sula bassana) can be seen here in the wake of a trawler off the Shetland Islands of Scotland.

Below: Not all seabirds feed on fish. This white-vented storm petrel (Oceanites gracilis) is feeding on planktonic debris, while paddling with its feet on the surface of the sea.

Right: All seabirds are forced back to land to breed, and some long-distance travellers seek out remote oceanic islands for this purpose. Cliff faces and nearby offshore stacks are the next best thing for other seabird colonies, offering shelter from the elements, although there is also less protection from opportunistic nest raiders, such as the larger gulls. Seabirds usually return year after year to the same nesting grounds, but will abandon them if their fish stocks plummet.

Birdwatching tips

• Seabirds such as albatrosses are attracted to passing ships because of the food that is thrown overboard. This means they are relatively easy to locate in certain areas – for example near shipping lanes.

• Ornithologists can often take trips on local boats to view seabird colonies. These and other sea crossings may present a good opportunity to watch birds feeding out at sea.

• If you are prone to seasickness, don't forget to take medication beforehand if you think you may feel ill on a trip.

• Binoculars can easily be lost overboard from a small boat in choppy seas. Always sling them (and any camera equipment) around your neck, rather than simply holding them in your hands.

Typical sightings in seas and oceans, depending to some extent on location:
• Auks
• Gannets
• Albatrosses
• Petrels

Below: For most ornithologists, organized charter boat trips present the only way to reach seabird colonies.

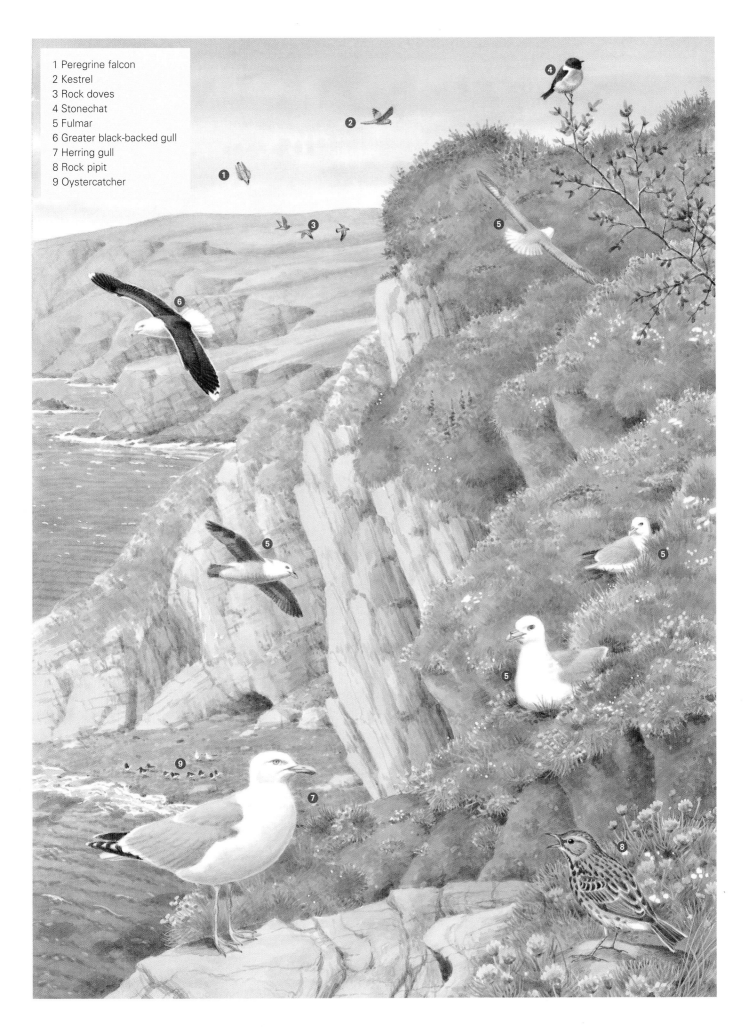

1 Peregrine falcon
2 Kestrel
3 Rock doves
4 Stonechat
5 Fulmar
6 Greater black-backed gull
7 Herring gull
8 Rock pipit
9 Oystercatcher

SEASHORE AND ESTUARY

Tidal rhythms have a significant impact on the habits of birds found on seashores and estuaries. These birds usually group together to feed on mudflats and sandbars that are uncovered at low tide. As the incoming tide encroaches, the birds are forced to retreat to the shoreline.

Gulls typify the image of the seashore more than any other group of birds, being a familiar sight on coasts the world over. These adaptable birds also venture well inland, especially to locations where food is available, such as public parks with ponds and even the less salubrious surroundings of refuse dumps.

Above: Sanderlings (Calidris alba) demonstrate the features of a typical wader. The daily lives of such birds are directly influenced by the movements of the tide.

Below: The appearance of black-headed gulls (Larus ridibundus) differs subtly between the seasons. In winter, the marked black plumage on the crown is reduced to a thin crescent of black which sits on either side of the head.

Lifestyle and feeding

Wading birds that frequent seashores typically have relatively long legs compared with perching birds, which enable them to walk through shallow water. Their narrow bills allow them to probe for invertebrates concealed in the mud. Some waders have evolved more specialized feeding habits, which are reflected in the shape of their bills. The oystercatcher (*Haematopus ostralegus*), for example, has a chisel-like tip to its bill that allows it to split open mollusc shells.

Shorebirds feed on a range of creatures, and can therefore be sighted further inland, even if only seeking sanctuary from storms. Some shorebirds are migratory, spending summer as far north as the Arctic Circle before heading south for winter again.

Breeding habits

Many birds that live close to the shoreline have to breed in the open. The eggs and chicks of such species,

which include curlews (*Numenius arquata*) have markings that conceal them well among the sand or pebbles. Even the coloring of the adult birds often helps to conceal their presence, with typical shades of grey, brown and white plumage merging into the background of the shoreline.

Within the tropics, a number of waterbirds have adapted to living in coastal mangrove forests, the roots of which are submerged by the incoming tide. They include some of the most spectacular members of the group, such as the pink-backed pelican (*Pelecanus rufescens*), which capitalizes on the abundance of cover, food and water in the mangroves to breed.

Right: The day-to-day distribution of seashore and estuarine birds is likely to be influenced by the weather. If conditions are stormy, birds often retreat to estuaries and coastal lagoons; in icy winter weather, a variety of unexpected species may be seen at estuaries, since these stretches of water do not freeze over, unlike surrounding areas of freshwater such as lakes.

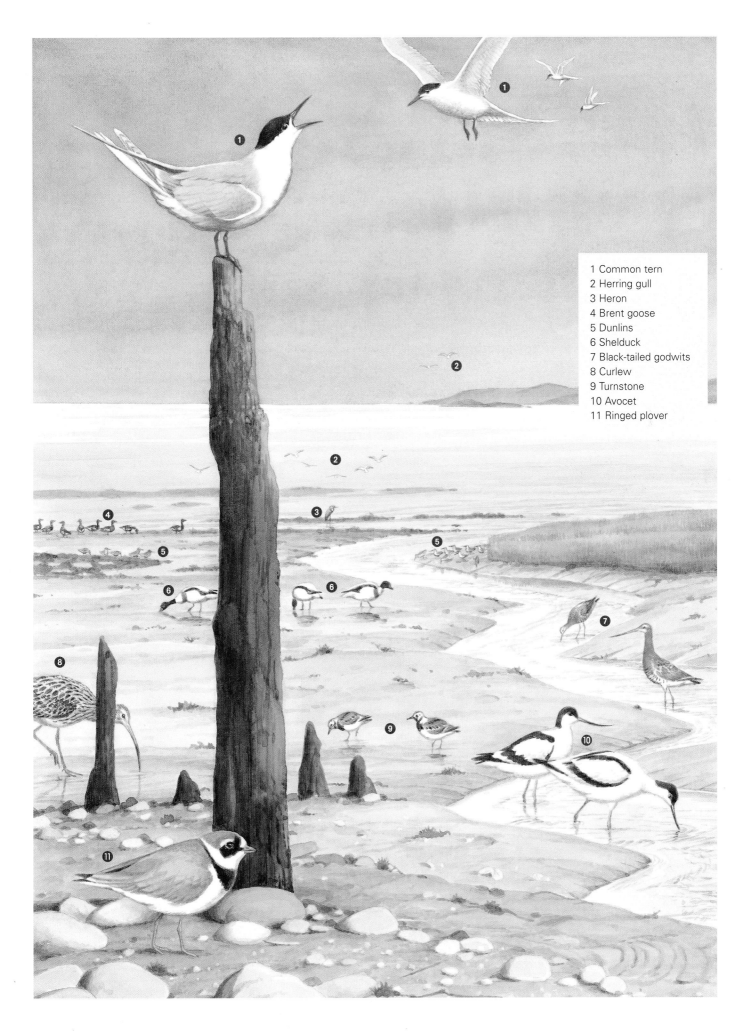

1 Common tern
2 Herring gull
3 Heron
4 Brent goose
5 Dunlins
6 Shelduck
7 Black-tailed godwits
8 Curlew
9 Turnstone
10 Avocet
11 Ringed plover

FRESHWATER LAKES, PONDS AND RIVERS

The speed of the water flow in freshwater habitats has a direct impact on the vegetation that grows there, which in turn influences the types of birds that may be seen. Some birds are drawn to lakes, ponds and rivers mainly for food, whereas others seek sanctuary from would-be predators there.

A wide variety of birds can be encountered by lakes, ponds and rivers, but not all are easy to observe. In areas of slow-flowing or still, shallow water where reed beds are well established, rails of various types (Rallidae) are often present, but these birds are shy by nature. Their mottled plumage provides camouflage, while their slim, tall body shape coupled with long, narrow toes allows them to move quietly through the vegetation.

Finding food

Many birds of prey hunt in freshwater habitats, swooping low over the water to seize fish by day and even at night. Fishing owls (*Scotopelia*) have sharp spines on the undersides of their feet that allow them to tighten their grip on fish hooked by their sharp talons. Other hunters rely on different strategies to catch food. Herons (Ardeidae) wait in the shallows and seize fish that swim in range of their sharp, powerful bills. Some fish-eating birds, notably some kingfishers (Alcedinidae), dive to seize their prey, which they may feed to their young in river bank nests.

Nesting

Some birds are drawn to lakes and rivers not so much by food but by nesting opportunities. Swallows (*Hirundo rustica*) collect damp mud from the

Below: The keen eyesight, long legs and prominent bill of birds such as this yellow-billed stork (Mycteria ibis) *help them to hunt and feed in freshwater habitats.*

Above: A sharp bill, narrow head and powerful neck mean that birds such as the red-necked grebe (Podiceps grisegena) *are well equipped to seize aquatic prey.*

water's edge to make their nests, and may also catch midges flying above the water. Most birds that actually nest by ponds and rivers seek seclusion when breeding. They hide their nest away, or make it hard to reach by choosing a spot surrounded by water, while taking care to avoid sites that may flood. Mute swans (*Cygnus olor*) construct large nests, which restricts their choice of sites. Both sexes, but especially the cob (male), defend the nest ferociously. These largish birds are capable of inflicting painful, damaging blows with

Below: An African jacana (Actophilornis africanus) *on a hippopotamus. This bird's long toes support its weight when walking over lily pads, so it does not sink down.*

their wings on would-be wild predators, dogs or even people who venture too close.

Birdwatching tips
• Patience is essential when watching freshwater birds, as many species are shy and easily frightened away.
• Certain localities, such as large lakes and gravel pits, are particularly good for spotting waterfowl in winter. Check local details in field guides or websites.
• Quietly paddling a canoe up a river can be a good way to spot birds, but plan carefully and be alert to possible dangers, such as strong currents, weirs or waterfalls on the route.
• Take great care near rivers when there is a risk of flooding, such as after heavy rain.

Typical sightings by lakes, ponds and rivers, depending on location:
• Ducks, geese and swans
• Rails
• Herons
• Birds of prey

Right: Lakes provide a range of different benefits for birds, ranging from calm, open water in which to swim, to the dense cover provided by reedbeds at the perimeter. The narrow body shape of birds such as crakes (Rallidae) *allows them to move easily through the dense vegetation, while taller reeds further inland make excellent vantage points for kingfishers* (Cerylidae) *spotting prey.*

1 Crowned cranes
2 Pied kingfisher
3 Open-bill stork
4 Fish eagle
5 Malachite kingfisher
6 Egyptian geese
7 Darter
8 Western reef heron
9 Cattle egret
10 Long-tailed cormorant
11 Great white pelican
12 African spoonbill
13 Goliath heron
14 Jacana
15 Black crake
16 Yellow-billed stork

TEMPERATE WOODLAND

The temperate woodlands of the Northern Hemisphere have altered significantly over time owing to climate change, receding in cold periods and expanding in warmer eras. Coniferous forests extend north to the treeless area known as the tundra, where it is too cold for even hardy trees to grow.

Bird life in coniferous forests is less varied than in deciduous, broad-leaved woodlands, largely because there are fewer feeding opportunities. A variety of species opt to live in this cooler habitat, however.

Coniferous woodlands

One resident is the spotted nutcracker (*Nucifraga caryocatactes*) of European and Asian forests. Their pointed bills allow these specialized members of the crow family to extract the seeds from pine cones very effectively.

The food supply in this habitat is not guaranteed, however. There are barren years when the trees do not produce as many cones as usual, forcing the birds to abandon their regular haunts and fly elsewhere. These unpredictable movements, known as irruptions, occur when birds suddenly appear in large numbers outside their normal range, searching for alternative sources of food. They later disappear

Below: Some predatory birds have adapted to life in temperate forests, especially owls such as this Tengmalm's owl (Aegolius funereus). These hunters mainly feed on rodents.

Above: Ground birds such as the capercaillie (Tetrao urogallus) breed on the ground, concealing their presence as far as possible. Their chicks are able to move immediately after they hatch out.

just as suddenly as they arrived, and may not return again for years. In northerly areas the landscape is covered in snow for much of the winter. Some species, including various corvids and woodpeckers, prepare for the cold weather by burying stores of nuts or hiding them in trees.

Owls are frequently found in coniferous forests, preying on the rodents that can be quite plentiful there. However, owls may also be forced to hunt elsewhere if the numbers of their prey plummet, as occasionally happens when there is a shortage of pine cones.

Deciduous woodlands

A greater variety of feeding opportunities exists for birds in deciduous forests. Such woodland is more open, which means that there is a significant understorey of vegetation and insects are more plentiful. Migratory birds take advantage of the feeding opportunities in these forests in summer. Ground birds of various types, including Eurasian woodcocks (*Scolopax rusticola*), are also found here. During the breeding season, the males become territorial and are often highly active at dusk. These birds eat a

Above: A pileated woodpecker (Dryocopus pileatus) male returns to the nest site. Trees provide relatively safe nesting havens, especially for birds such as woodpeckers that can create their own nesting holes.

variety of foods, ranging from seeds to berries and invertebrates, depending on the time of year.

Birdwatching tips
• Spring is a good time to spot birds in deciduous woodlands, before the trees are covered in leaves.
• Woodlands and particularly coniferous forests can be disorientating, so take a map and compass if you're going any distance in case you lose your bearings.
• In summer, woodland glades attract invertebrates, which in turn attract insectivorous birds in search of prey.
• Stand quietly in woodlands and listen – the song of woodland birds helps to reveal their presence.

Typical sightings in temperate woodlands, depending to some extent on location:
• Woodpeckers
• Finches
• Owls
• Warblers

Right: In many ways, temperate woodland is an ideal avian habitat during the warm months of the year, providing a wide range of food, excellent cover and a variety of nesting sites. During the winter months, however, life here can become much harsher. Once the leaves have fallen, the birds will be much more conspicuous, and food is likely to be scarcer. Survival will become even harder if snow blankets the ground.

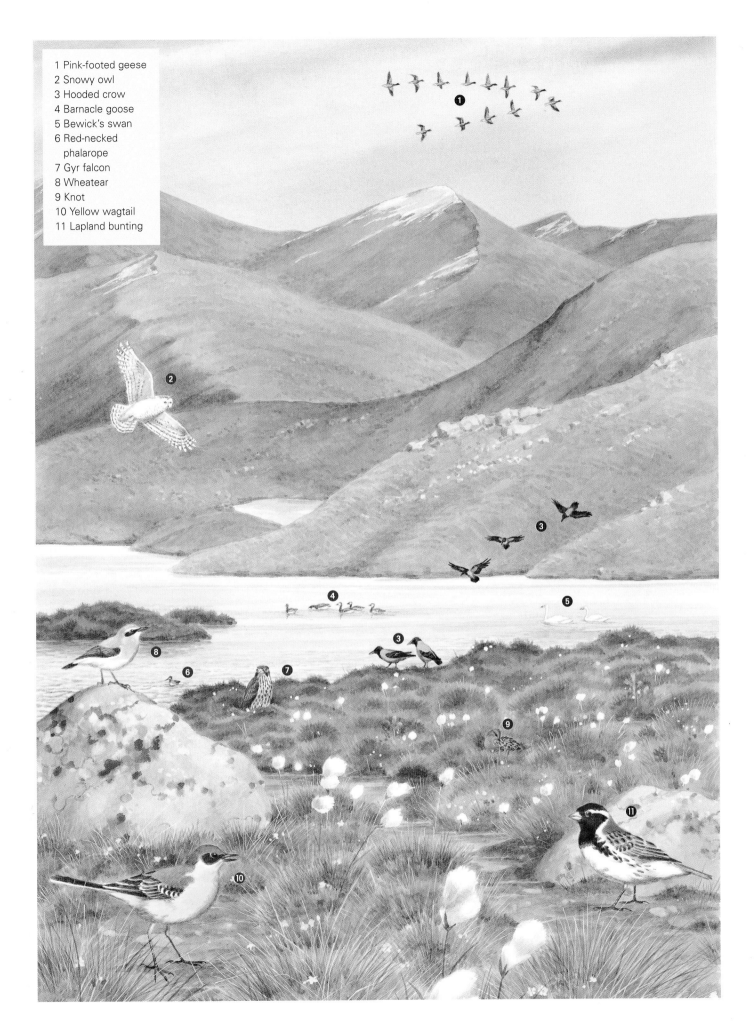

1 Pink-footed geese
2 Snowy owl
3 Hooded crow
4 Barnacle goose
5 Bewick's swan
6 Red-necked
  phalarope
7 Gyr falcon
8 Wheatear
9 Knot
10 Yellow wagtail
11 Lapland bunting

GRASSLAND, STEPPE AND MOORLAND

Open grasslands offer relatively little cover to birds, and some are harsh, treeless places where both water and food may be scarce. A number of birds found in these areas are ground-dwellers, and they are often well camouflaged, which makes them hard to spot unless flushed from their hiding places.

Moors and grasslands are among the best habitats in which to spot predatory birds as they fly overhead seeking live quarry or carcasses to scavenge. Prey species are also present in numbers, but they are more difficult to spot because of their camouflage.

Spotting predatory birds

Large predators and scavengers such as condors (Cathartidae) fly high over grasslands, utilizing the warm air

Left: The northern wheatear (Oenanthe oenanthe) *is a migratory species, breeding in Europe and wintering in Africa.*

Above: Open country predators such as this golden eagle (Aquila chrysaetos) *benefit from keen eyesight, which enables them to spot quarry on the ground while in flight.*

currents known as thermals, which allow them to remain airborne with minimal effort. Smaller hunters such as hawks swoop down much lower over the open countryside as they search for the small mammals or birds that form the basis of their diet.

Survival of terrestrial birds

Many birds occupying grassland areas have evolved either to become very large, as in the case of the ostrich (*Struthio camellus*), or are small and inconspicuous as increased protection against predators. Many terrestrial birds rely on their ability to remain undetected if danger threatens, only taking flight as a last resort. Skylarks (*Alauda arvensis*) have developed an unusual way of drawing a would-be predator away from their nest site by feigning an injury, often to the wing.

These birds have also been disrupted by human intervention, however, such as the cultivation of open fields which

has disturbed the nesting patterns of both skylarks and corncrakes *(Crex crex)*. Furthermore, insecticides have reduced their natural food resources, which are vital to the successful rearing of their young.

Moorland camouflage

On moorlands and steppes the weather can become cold and snowy in winter. Some of the birds found in this terrain undergo a seasonal moult at the onset of winter, from which they emerge transformed by lighter-coloured plumage to help conceal their presence.

Birdwatching tips

• Seek a good vantage point to increase your chances of spotting and following birds of prey.
• You will need a pair of powerful binoculars in grassland environments, as you will be combing relatively large and distant expanses of sky and land in search of birds.
• Use whatever natural cover is available to conceal your presence, such as tall vegetation and outcropping rocks.
• Horse riding can be a good way to cover long distances in grasslands and yet have a reasonable chance of spotting bird life, because birds are often less fearful of people on horseback.

Typical sightings in grassland habitats, depending to some extent on location:
• Eagles
• Vultures
• Grouse
• Hawks

Right: Open countryside can range from bleak moorland or arid steppeland to agricultural areas where trees have been cleared to create fields. These may then be ploughed to grow cereal crops, or left as meadows which can support a rich diversity of plant and animal life, including birds, although any resulting avian life may not be especially conspicuous to the observer. Grasslands offer better prospects of spotting birds of prey, however, since they are forced to spend relatively long periods on the wing scanning the ground for food.

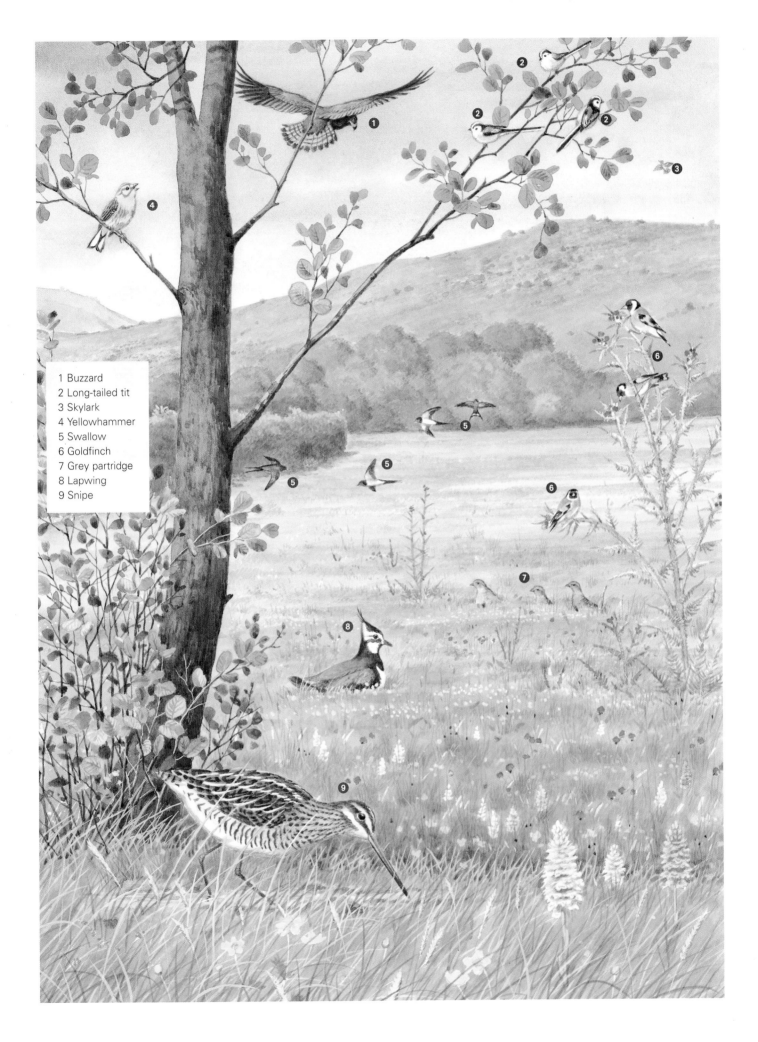

1 Buzzard
2 Long-tailed tit
3 Skylark
4 Yellowhammer
5 Swallow
6 Goldfinch
7 Grey partridge
8 Lapwing
9 Snipe

URBAN LIFE

Some birds display a remarkable ability to adapt to modern life, occurring right in the centre of cities.
They use buildings for nesting and, in the case of birds of prey, as vantage points for hunting, just as they
would use trees or rocky crags in the wild. City parks, in particular, have become major refuges for birds.

Cities tend to be slightly warmer than the surrounding countryside, and this warm microclimate offers a number of advantages for birds. Drinking water is less likely to freeze in cold weather, and in spring, insects are more abundant at an earlier time, as plants bud and grow more quickly because of the warmth.

Residents and visitors

Some birds live permanently in cities, taking advantage of parks, whereas

Above: Out of all birds, the feral pigeon (Columba livia) has adapted best to urban life, to the extent that it is now a common sight in cities around the world.

Below: Cattle egrets (Bubulcus ibis) have proved remarkably adaptable in their invasion of cities, and are often found scavenging around markets or refuse dumps. They can prove surprisingly bold in such surroundings, unfazed even by the presence of vehicles.

Above: Buildings can represent safe localities for nest-building. White storks (Ciconia ciconia) such as these have nested on town roofs for centuries in some parts of their range.

others are more casual visitors, flying in to roost at night from outlying areas, or pausing here on migration. Deserted buildings offer a snug and relatively safe retreat for birds that roost in flocks, whereas birds of prey seek the inaccessible ledges of high-rise buildings. The abundance of feral pigeons (*Columba livia*) in built-up areas attracts peregrine falcons (*Falco peregrinus*), proving that they are just as adaptable as their prey. The falcons may keep pigeon populations in check, but if not, their numbers can be also curbed by feeding them with corn, which acts as a contraceptive.

A life above the bustle of city streets generally offers predatory species a fairly safe existence, compared with more rural areas where they risk being shot illegally. There are still dangers lurking on the city streets, however. High-rise office blocks with large expanses of glass can lure birds to a fatal collision.

Migrating birds still pass through cities on occasions, notably huge flocks of common starlings (*Sturnus vulgaris*). These congregate not just in city parks, but also roost on buildings and tree-lined streets when breaking their journey, creating a noisy chatter and plenty of mess.

Birdwatching tips
• City parks offer the best chances of spotting the largest number of species in urban environments, particularly if there is a sizeable pond or lake.
• Early morning is a good time to spot birds at close quarters in cities, before many people are on the streets.
• Don't forget about the dangers of traffic in your enthusiasm to spot particular birds.
• Join the local ornithological society to gain insight into the more unusual species found in local towns and cities.

Typical sightings in urban environments, depending to some extent on location:
• Falcons
• Owls
• Pigeons and doves
• Gulls

Right: Urbanization has inevitably influenced resident avian populations by altering the surrounding habitat. Only opportunists such as pigeons – with their extremely adaptable dietary habits – will actually thrive in crowded city centres, but a much wider variety of bird life can be seen in city parks. Various species of waterfowl, for example, have been introduced to man-made ponds and lakes, while coastal birds such as gulls will also scavenge in this habitat.

1 Jackdaw
2 Starling
3 Pigeon
4 Magpie
5 Black-headed gull
6 Coot
7 Mute swan
8 Tufted duck
9 Mallard
10 Pintail
11 Wigeon
12 Goldeneye
13 House sparrow
14 Wood duck

GARDENS

An amazingly wide variety of birds have been recorded as regular garden visitors. It is possible to observe as many as 40 species regularly visiting bird tables in urban areas of north-western Europe. Feeding stations undoubtedly help to draw birds to gardens, but birds also visit as part of their natural behaviour.

Tidy, immaculately manicured gardens generally support less bird life than well-established gardens with plenty of mature shrubs that can be used for roosting and nesting. If there are stands of trees nearby, or even just lining the road outside, the range of birds visiting the garden will increase, and larger species will become more common. Artificial nesting sites, such as nest boxes of various types and sizes, can also help to increase the variety and numbers of birds that visit gardens regularly.

Birds face a major danger in gardens in the guise of the domestic cat. Huge numbers of individuals fall victim to these pets annually. The majority of the casualties are young fledglings, which lack the awareness and caution of adult birds. In areas where the cat population is especially high, there

Above: Bird tables and feeders help to attract birds into gardens by providing them with additional food sources. These are especially valuable during cold winter weather.

may be local declines in bird numbers. However, studies suggest that bird populations do not seem to be adversely affected by cats overall.

Helpers and pests

Birds are often regarded as gardeners' friends because they help to control the number of invertebrate pests in gardens. For example, tits (*Parus*) eat aphids on rose bushes, and thrushes (*Turdus*) hunt snails. At certain times of year, however, some birds can themselves become pests. Pigeons (*Columba*), in particular, often dig up newly planted seeds and eat them before they can germinate, unless the seeds are protected in some way. Later in the year, some species eat ripening berries.

Residents and migrants

Some birds are resident in garden settings throughout the year. Others are temporary visitors, migrating to warmer climates for the winter period. Many warblers (Sylviidae) can be seen in northern Europe for only part of the year, before heading south to winter in Africa. At this time, migrants from further north may descend on gardens to replace the species that have left, as

occurs with the fieldfare (*Turdus pilaris*). Studies provide clear evidence that actual shifts in the behaviour and distribution of birds are currently occurring because of the availability of garden habitat and the provision of food there. The Eurasian blackbird (*Turdus merula*), a native of field and woodland, has become a common sight in gardens, while the Eurasian collared dove (*Streptopelia decaocto*), native to India, has undoubtedly benefited from bird table fare as it has spread from Asia into parts of Europe.

Above: Fieldfares (Turdus pilaris) *arrive from their northerly breeding grounds to winter in European gardens and farmland, where they like to feed on fallen fruit. These thrushes can be identified by their harsh, chuckling calls.*

Right: In many respects, gardens offer an ideal habitat for birds. Food is readily available in these surroundings, as well as trees and shrubs, which provide good opportunities for roosting and nesting. Unfortunately, gardens can often be dangerous places for birds to visit, thanks to the popularity of cats as pets. Nor are cats the only danger in this type of habitat. Predatory birds, notably magpies (Pica pica), *will raid the nests of smaller birds, taking both eggs and chicks.*

1 Rooks
2 Spotted flycatcher
3 Collared dove
4 Chaffinch
5 Robin
6 Mistle thrush
7 Blackbird
8 Blue tit
9 Wren
10 Dunnock

ENDANGERED SPECIES AND CONSERVATION

It has been estimated that three-quarters of the world's birds may come under threat in the 21st century. Habitat destruction poses the most serious danger, so conservationists are striving to preserve bird habitats worldwide. Direct intervention of various kinds is also used to ensure the survival of particular species.

Around the world, threats to birds are varied and complex, but most are linked to human interference in the ecosystem, and will thus continue to grow as human populations increase.

Habitat destruction

Habitat destruction includes the deforestation of the world's tropical rainforests, which host a wide variety of birds, and also the conversion of many grassland areas into crop fields or livestock pasture. The first casualties of habitat destruction are often species with specialized feeding or nesting requirements, which cannot easily adapt to change.

In recent years, there have been a number of instances of opportunistic species adapting and thriving in altered habitats. One example is the common mynah (*Acridotheres tristis*), whose natural distribution is centred on India but has been introduced to many other localities worldwide, often to control locust numbers. Its range now includes southern Africa and the Seychelles.

Below: The waldrapp, or bald ibis (Geronticus eremita), *is now the subject of intense conservation efforts, with captive-breeding programmes in force to build on its numbers.*

Above: Aquatic birds, such as these wattled cranes (Bugeranus carunculatus) *are often vulnerable to marshland drainage schemes or commercial developments.*

Generally, the diversity of bird life in an area declines drastically when the land is modified or cleared.

Hunting and pollution

Unregulated hunting of adult birds, eggs or young threatens a variety of species worldwide. The birds may be killed for their meat or feathers, or captured live and sold through the pet trade. In many countries, laws are now in place to protect rare species, but hunting and trading still go on illegally.

Overfishing is a related hazard facing seabirds, especially now that trawling methods have become so efficient. Global shortages of fish stocks are forcing fishermen to target fish that had previously been of little commercial value, but that are an important part of seabirds' diets.

In agricultural areas, pesticides and herbicides sprayed on farmers' fields decimate bird populations by eliminating their plant or animal food supplies. Deliberate or accidental contamination of the soil, air or water by industrial chemicals is another hazard, while in the oceans, seabirds are killed by dumped toxins and oil spills. Disease is another major threat that may increase.

Climate change

In the near future, global warming caused by increased emissions of carbon dioxide and other gases is likely to impact on many bird habitats, and will almost certainly adversely affect birds' food supplies. If plants or other foods become unavailable in an area, birds must adapt their feeding habits or face extinction. As temperatures rise, the melting of the polar ice caps will threaten seabird populations by destroying their traditional nesting areas. Rising sea levels will also threaten low-lying wetlands favoured by wading birds.

Threats to island birds

Some of the world's most distinctive birds have evolved in relative isolation on islands. Unfortunately, these species are also extremely vulnerable to changes in their environment, partly because their populations are small. One of the greatest threats comes from

Above: This guillemot (Uria aalge) killed in Scottish waters is just one of the countless avian victims claimed by oil spillages each year. Large spills of oil can have devastating effects on whole populations.

introduced predators, particularly domestic cats. Most famously, off the coast of New Zealand in 1894, the resident lighthouse keeper's cat killed the last Stephen Island wren (Xenicus lyalli), which was unique to this habitat, before any official record of the species had been made.

Cats are not the only introduced predators that can cause serious harm to avian populations. Grazing animals such as goats, introduced to islands by passing ships to provide future crews with fresh meat, have frequently destroyed the native vegetation, so reducing the birds' food supply. Rats and pigs threaten ground-nesting birds as they will prey on both their eggs and even young chicks.

Today, control of harmful introduced species is helping to protect surviving populations of endangered island birds, but sadly for some species this action has come too late to save them from total extinction.

Conservation and captive-breeding

Preserving habitat is the best and most cost-effective way to ensure the survival of all the birds that frequent a particular ecosystem. A worldwide network of national parks and reserves

now helps to protect at least part of many birds' habitats. In addition, conservationists may take a variety of direct measures to safeguard the future of particular species, such as breeding in captivity, or translocation. The latter method sees conservation officials remove the youngest chicks from wild nests, which are subsequently reared to independence and released into a new location, where it is hoped they will thrive. Using this approach, golden eagles (Aquila chrysaetos) have been translocated to Ireland from their native home in the Scottish highlands.

Artificially or naturally fertilized eggs can be transferred to incubators to be hatched, effectively doubling the number of chicks that can be reared. This is because removing the eggs often stimulates the hen to lay again more quickly than usual. Hand-rearing chicks on formulated diets helps to ensure the survival of the young once hatched. When hand-reared chicks are later released into the wild, it is vital that they bond with their own species and retain their natural fear of people, so glove puppets shaped like the parent birds are often used to feed the chicks.

Reintroduction programmes

Breeding endangered species is relatively easy compared with the difficulties of reintroducing a species to

Above: Glove puppets resembling the parent bird's head are often used when hand-rearing chicks such as this peregrine falcon (Falco peregrinus), to encourage the birds to bond with their own kind when eventually released.

an area of its former habitat. The cost of such reintroduction programmes is often very high. Staff are needed not only to look after the aviary stock and rear the chicks, but also to carry out habitat studies. These assess the dangers that the birds will face after release and pinpoint release sites. The released birds must then be monitored, which may include fitting them with radio transmitters.

Ecotourism

Working with local people and gaining their support is often essential to the long-term successes of conservation initiatives. On Mauritius, an island home to unique indigenous species such as the echo parakeet (Psittacula echo) and the pink pigeon (Columba mayeri), international assistance from organisations such as the Jersey Wildlife Preservation Trust has helped both to increase the numbers of these critically endangered birds, and also to make local people more aware of the significance of their native wildlife as part of the island's heritage. It has also raised the profile of these particular species on a global scale, increasing the flux of tourists to this island and bringing in some much needed foreign currency to boost the local economy.

Left: Around 20% of the world's surviving rainforest is located in Africa, such as the Uluguru montane forests in Tanzania. Yet ongoing clearance of land continues to threaten the many birds living there.

CLASSIFICATION

The way in which different birds are grouped is known as classification. This is not only helpful in terms of distinguishing individual species and those that are closely related, but it also enables wider assessments of relationships between larger groups to be made.

Interest in how best to group birds into distinct categories is nothing new. It dates back nearly 2,500 years to the ancient Greeks, when an early method of classification was developed by the philosopher Aristotle. He sought to group living creatures on the basis of differences in their lifestyles, rather than on the basis of anatomical distinctions, which are favoured today. The first modern attempt to trace relationships between birds was made by Sir Francis Willoughby, in a book entitled *Ornithologia*, which was published in 1676. Willoughby saw the need for what was essentially an identification key that would enable readers to find an unknown bird by means of special tables devised for this purpose.

Willoughby's work concentrated solely on birds, but it was actually a Swedish botanist, Carl von Linné (also known as Linnaeus), who devised the universal system of classification that

Above: The so-called nominate subspecies of the African grey parrot – Psittacus erithacus erithacus.

Below: This is the timneh subspecies of the grey parrot, known scientifically as Psittacus erithacus timneh.

is now known as the Linnean System. Linné relied primarily on the physical similarities between living organisms as the basis for grouping them, laying the foundations for the science of classification, which is now known as systematics. He refined this approach through a series of new editions of his classic work *Systema Naturae*, which was originally published in 1735.

Linné's system operates through a series of ranks, creating what is sometimes described as a hierarchal method. Starting from a very general base, the ranks become increasingly specific, splitting into smaller groups, until finally, individual types of birds can be identified. One advantage of this system is that when a new species is discovered, it can be fitted easily into this existing framework.

New advances

While Linné and successive generations of taxonomists relied on physical similarities, the use of DNA analysis is currently transforming our understanding of the natural world. By comparing sequences of the genetic material DNA, it is possible for ornithologists to investigate which birds share DNA sequences that suggest a close relationship. This method of study is set to revolutionize taxonomy and is already leading to numerous revisions of the existing classification of birds.

How the system works

Birds, as animals, belong to the Kingdom Animalia, and, having backbones, they are members of the phylum Chordata, which includes all vertebrates. The class Aves is the first division at which birds are separated from other vertebrates such as mammals. Birds alone comprise this major grouping, which is subdivided into smaller categories called orders.

*Above: This is the African race of ring-necked parakeet (*Psittacula krameri krameri*). The plumage is of a more yellowish shade than its Indian relative, and the bill is darker.*

It is then a matter of tracking an individual species down through the various ranks of classification. For example, the classificatory breakdown of the grey parrot is as follows:
Order: Psittaciformes
Family: Psittacidae
Genus: *Psittacus*
Species: *Psittacus erithacus*
Subspecies: *Psittacus erithacus erithacus, Psittacus erithacus timneh*
If you are unsure where you are in the ranking, the way in which the names are written gives a clear indication. The names of orders end in "-formes", while family names terminate with "-idae". At or below genus level, all names are italicized, with the genus comprising one or more species. The scientific name of a species always consists of two descriptions, with the genus names being written first. Species are the basic fundamental level in the taxonomic tree, enabling particular types of birds to be named individually. Members of a particular species generally identify with each

other and do not normally interbreed with other species. However, if interbreeding does occur, the resulting offspring are known as hybrids.

At the most specific level of the taxonomic tree are subspecies: closely related forms of the same species that are nevertheless distinctive enough to be identified separately. These are often defined on the basis of their size, although also because of distinct differences in coloration. In the case of the grey parrot (*Psittacus erithacus*) given above, the so-called nominate form, which is the first form to have been recognized, is *Psittacus erithacus erithacus*, as indicated by a repetition of the so-called trivial name *erithacus*. The subspecies timneh (which can be written in an abbreviated form *P. e. timneh* in the context of the nominate subspecies) is recognizable in this instance because of its smaller size, significantly darker grey coloration and maroon rather than red tail feathers.

It was Linné himself who devised this method of distinguishing between such closely related individuals, first describing it in 1758. His method is sometimes known as the trinomial

system, thanks to its use of three names in these cases.

What's in a name?
Even the choice of scientific names is not random. They can give an insight into a bird's appearance or distribution, often based on Latin. The name *flavinucha*, for example, indicates yellow plumage around the neck; the description *peruviana* in the case of the parrot-billed seed-eater (*Sporophila peruviana*) indicates the bird's distribution in South America. In a few instances, the species' description features a person's name, for example *Chloebia gouldiae* – the Gouldian finch – which the noted naturalist and explorer John Gould named after his wife Elizabeth, because of its beauty. In order to be recognized as a species, an example of the bird concerned, known as the "type specimen", has to be held in a museum collection, enabling a detailed description to be written up as part of the identification process.

*Below: Subtle but consistent differences in appearance allow the various races, or "subspecies", to be distinguished. The Indian race of ring-necked parakeet (*Psittacula krameri manillensis*) is seen here. It has a bright red bill and greener overall plumage.*

DIRECTORY OF BIRDS

Identifying birds in many cases is not easy, particularly if you have only a relatively brief sighting. This part of the book has therefore been divided into the key habitat groups – including sea, estuarine, freshwater, woodland, open country and urban locations – designed to simplify the task of identification as much as possible by allowing you to link your sightings with the place in which you spotted the bird. It should be pointed out that this system is not infallible, as some birds are highly adaptable and range widely through different environments, but it is a useful starting point. Distribution maps accompanying all the illustrated entries provide a visual guide as to where exactly bird species are likely to be found within these regions, while the text indicates the various locations in which migratory species can be seen at differing times of the year.

The associated descriptions will help to clarify whether you have seen a cock bird or a hen, since there are often plumage differences between the sexes. Other information in these fact boxes about habitat, feeding and breeding behaviour should provide further help when it comes to identifying a particular bird. A bird's general shape, its habits, and the characteristic way in which it moves, all add up to what birdwatchers call its "jizz", which can help to pinpoint birds even from a tiny speck in the sky or a dark shape scuttling behind a hedge.

Not every species within the terrain of Great Britain, Europe and Africa is covered, but the representative sample featured in the following pages – which are grouped with similar "types" or family members – should at least allow you to narrow down the search. Browsing through these pages also affords an opportunity to learn more about the diverse avian life of these continents, ranging from the hornbills of the west African rainforests, to the eider ducks breeding within the Arctic Circle, not overlooking the many predatory birds and Columbiforms that have made a home in our city centres.

Left: Bee-eaters (Meropidae) are colourful and social birds, and species can be found in both Europe and Africa. They live in colonies, carving out nesting holes in sandy river banks with their long, pointed bills. Bee-eaters feed mainly on bees and wasps, and rub their insect prey on the ground before consuming it, either to remove the sting or kill them outright.

BIRDS OF GREAT BRITAIN
EUROPE & AFRICA

The distribution of birds occurring in this part of the world, especially those found in Europe, often extends eastwards into Asia as well. Many northerly species also undergo regular seasonal movements in response to the climate, overwintering in more southerly latitudes, with some even flying as far as southern Africa. Those groups of birds most commonly associated with tropical areas – such as parrots, for example – are poorly represented in this region of the world, partly because of the absence of suitable feeding opportunities in Europe. Urban development in this part of the world has also had a marked impact on the distribution of a number of species, and some have adapted to urban environments better than others. Human involvement has also seen the introduction of avian species into Europe from outside their natural range, often for sporting purposes, as in the case of various species of pheasants and partridges.

Above from left: kestrel (Falco tinnunculus), *eagle owl* (Bubo bubo), *kingfisher* (Alcedo atthis).

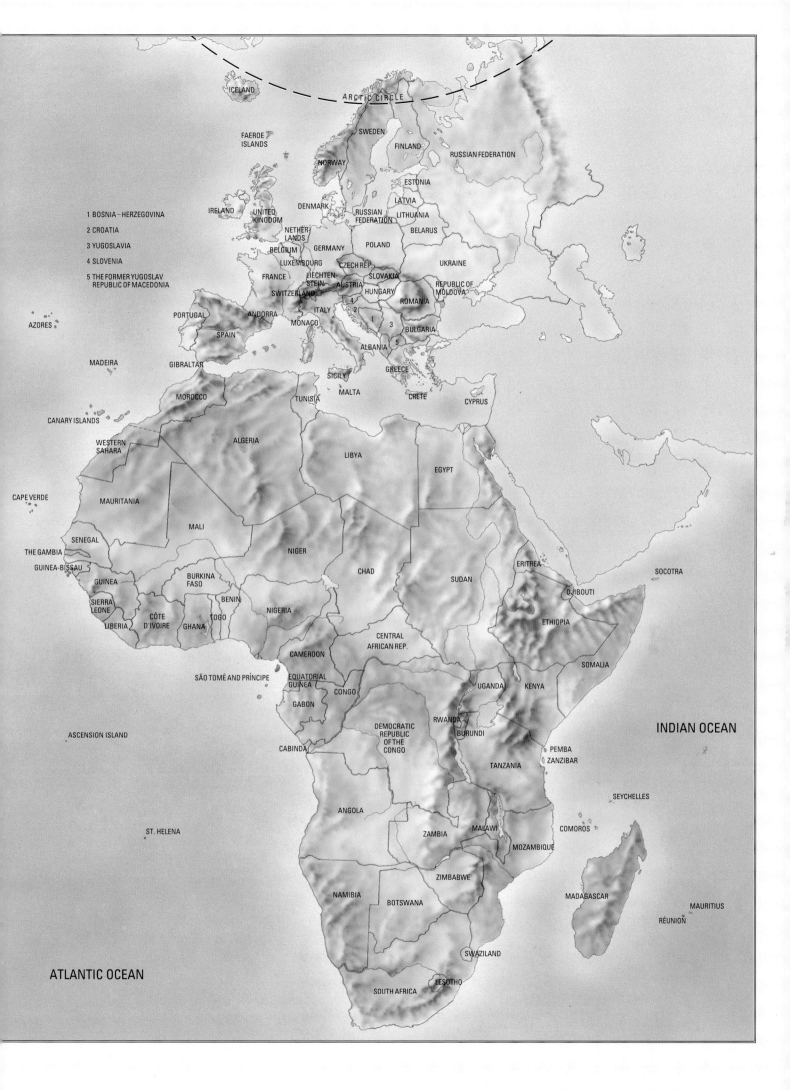

ICELAND

ARCTIC CIRCLE

FAEROE
ISLANDS

SWEDEN

FINLAND

NORWAY

RUSSIAN FEDERATION

ESTONIA

LATVIA

1 BOSNIA – HERZEGOVINA

2 CROATIA

3 YUGOSLAVIA

4 SLOVENIA

5 THE FORMER YUGOSLAV
   REPUBLIC OF MACEDONIA

IRELAND

UNITED
KINGDOM

DENMARK

RUSSIAN
FEDERATION

LITHUANIA

BELARUS

NETHER-
LANDS

POLAND

BELGIUM

GERMANY

LUXEMBOURG

CZECH REP.

UKRAINE

FRANCE

LIECHTEN-
STEIN

SLOVAKIA

SWITZERLAND

AUSTRIA

HUNGARY

REPUBLIC OF
MOLDOVA

PORTUGAL

ANDORRA

4

ITALY

ROMANIA

MONACO

2

3

SPAIN

1

BULGARIA

AZORES

5

ALBANIA

MADEIRA

GIBRALTAR

SICILY

MALTA

GREECE

CRETE

CYPRUS

MOROCCO

TUNISIA

CANARY ISLANDS

WESTERN
SAHARA

ALGERIA

LIBYA

EGYPT

CAPE VERDE

MAURITANIA

MALI

SENEGAL

THE GAMBIA

NIGER

GUINEA-BISSAU

CHAD

SUDAN

ERITREA

SOCOTRA

GUINEA

BURKINA
FASO

DJIBOUTI

SIERRA
LEONE

BENIN

NIGERIA

ETHIOPIA

LIBERIA

CÔTE
D'IVOIRE

GHANA

TOGO

CENTRAL
AFRICAN REP.

CAMEROON

SOMALIA

SÃO TOMÉ AND PRÍNCIPE

EQUATORIAL
GUINEA

UGANDA

KENYA

CONGO

RWANDA

ASCENSION ISLAND

GABON

DEMOCRATIC
REPUBLIC
OF THE
CONGO

BURUNDI

INDIAN OCEAN

CABINDA

PEMBA

ZANZIBAR

TANZANIA

SEYCHELLES

ANGOLA

MALAWI

COMOROS

ST. HELENA

ZAMBIA

MOZAMBIQUE

ZIMBABWE

MADAGASCAR

MAURITIUS

NAMIBIA

BOTSWANA

RÉUNION

SWAZILAND

ATLANTIC OCEAN

LESOTHO

SOUTH AFRICA

SEABIRDS

Some seabirds have evolved to live largely on the wing. Others, such as the little auk, have adapted to a more aquatic lifestyle. The auks have sometimes been described as "penguins of the north", but they are not closely related to penguins, which are confined to the southern oceans, although their coloration is similar.

Gannet

Northern gannet *Sula bassana*

Distribution: Along the eastern seaboard of North America extending across the Atlantic via southern Greenland and Iceland beyond Norway, southwards through the Mediterranean down to the west coast of North Africa.
Size: 88–100cm (35–39in).
Habitat: Sea.
Nest: Usually on cliffs, built from seaweed and other marine debris held together by droppings.
Eggs: 1, whitish.
Food: Fish.

This species is the largest of all gannets and can weigh up to 3.6kg (8lb). It is the only member of this group found around the North Atlantic. These gannets are powerful in the air. Their keen eyesight allows them to detect shoals of fish such as herring and mackerel in the ocean below. When feeding, gannets dive down into a shoal, often from a considerable height, seizing fish from under the water. Their streamlined shape also enables them to swim. Breeding occurs in the spring when the birds form large colonies in which there is often a lot of squabbling. The young mature slowly, and are unlikely to breed until they are at least four years old.

Identification: Mainly white, aside from pale creamy yellow plumage on the head extending down the neck, and black flight feathers. Tail feathers are white, and the feet are dark grey. Sexes alike. Young birds are dark brown in colour.

Great skua

Catharacta skua

These large, powerfully built birds can sometimes look rather like buzzards in flight, soaring above the ocean. When landing on the sea, great skuas glide down and hover in an unusual way before actually touching down on the water. They are highly opportunistic feeders, catching fish themselves and also robbing other seabirds of their catches. These birds also eat carrion, and their diet tends to be most variable during the breeding period, when they spend time on land. At this time they may even be observed eating berries or catching small rodents.

Identification: Predominantly dull brown with lighter streaking and barring. Distinctive white wing flashes visible when in flight. Strong, powerful hooked bill and relatively short tail. Sexes similar but hens may have more yellowish-brown markings on the neck. Young birds have brown underparts.

Distribution: Ranges widely throughout the Atlantic Ocean.
Size: 50–58cm (20–23in).
Habitat: Sea and coast.
Nest: Depression on the ground.
Eggs: 2, olive grey to reddish brown with darker markings.
Food: Typically fish and carrion.

Manx shearwater (*Puffinus puffinus*): 35cm (14in)
Widely distributed through the North Atlantic, as far as the coast of Iceland and south through the North Sea to the eastern coast of Spain. Also ranges further south off the north-western coast of Africa, and the southern tip of the continent. Sooty black upperparts, white beneath, including the undertail coverts. Sexes alike.

Parasitic jaeger (Arctic skua, *Stercorarius parasiticus*): 44cm (17in)
Present in the Atlantic Ocean extending up to the Arctic, but usually wintering south of the Equator. Sleek, gull-like appearance with long, narrow tail extensions averaging nearly 9cm (3.5in) in the summer. Dark crown with greyish wings and tail and white underparts at this time. Also occurs as a dark morph, lacking white plumage. Young birds have a barred appearance. Sexes are alike.

Guillemot (*Uria aalge*): 46cm (18in)
Ranges from off the western coast of Iceland and Ireland south to Spain and east through the North Sea as far as Scandinavia. Rather penguin-like appearance when standing vertically, but unlike penguins, can fly. Black head, chest and back, with white underparts and some streaking on the flanks. Thin white band over each wing, just above the flight feathers. Narrow, pointed black bill. Sexes alike.

Razorbill (*Alca torda*): 43cm (17in)
Similar distribution to the guillemot, with which it may associate, but also extends further south to North Africa and the western Mediterranean. Rather similar in coloration to the guillemot, too, but easily discernible by the broad, flat bill that has a white horizontal stripe on it, and its longer tail. A white stripe also extends to the eyes. Sexes alike.

Puffin

Fratercula arctica

These auks have unmistakable bills, said to resemble those of parrots. Young puffins have much narrower and less brightly coloured bills than the adults. Puffins come ashore to nest in colonies on cliffs and coastal areas where they can breed largely hidden from predators. Sand eels figure prominently in their diet at this time, and adult birds often fly quite long distances to obtain food. When underwater, puffins use their wings like flippers, enabling them to swim faster. Adult birds fly back to their young with eels arranged in a row, hanging down each side of their bills. They can carry as many as ten fish at a time in this way.

Left: The appearance of the puffin's bill varies depending on the bird's age and the time of year.

Right: Puffins excavate nesting tunnels underground or use existing holes.

Distribution: Throughout the northern Atlantic, including Spitzbergen.
Size: 32cm (13in).
Habitat: Sea and coastal areas.
Nest: Underground burrows.
Eggs: 1, white.
Food: Fish.

Identification: Whitish sides to the face, with black extending back over the crown. Black neck, back and wings; underparts white, with a grey area on the flanks. Broad, flattened bill with red area running down its length and across the tip. Greyish base with yellow area intervening. Bill less brightly coloured and sides of the face greyish during the winter. Sexes alike.

Little auk

Alle alle

In spite of its relatively restricted distribution, the little auk is considered to be possibly the most numerous seabird in the world. It forms huge nesting colonies in the Arctic region during the brief summer, before heading south at the approach of winter as the sea starts to freeze. Little auks are often more likely to be spotted at this time of year, frequently flying very low over the waves or even through them on occasion. Sometimes, however, fierce storms make feeding virtually impossible, and in a weakened state, little auks are driven into coastal areas. This phenomenon is often described as a "wreck".

Identification: In summer plumage, the head and upper part of the chest are black. The back, wings and upper surface of the tail feathers are also black, aside from white streaks apparent over the wings. During the winter, the black on the face is broken by white, leaving a black band across the throat. The bill is small and black. Sexes alike.

Distribution: Icelandic coast to northern Scandinavia, across the North Sea to the coast of eastern England.
Size: 20cm (8in).
Habitat: Sea and coastal areas.
Nest: Cliffs or crevices.
Eggs: 1, pale blue.
Food: Microscopic plankton.

GULLS

Gulls are linked in many people's minds with the seaside, but some species have proved very adept at adjusting to living alongside people and generally profiting from this association. A number of different gulls have now spread to various inland localities. Shades of white and grey generally predominate in the plumage of these birds, making them quite easy to recognize.

Herring gull

Larus argentatus

These large gulls are often seen on fishing jetties and around harbours, searching for scraps. They have also moved inland and can be seen in areas such as rubbish dumps, where they scavenge for food, often in quite large groups. Herring gulls are noisy by nature, especially when breeding. They now frequently nest on rooftops in coastal towns and cities, a trend that began as recently as the 1940s in Britain. Pairs can become very aggressive at breeding time, swooping menacingly on people who venture close to the nest site or even to the chicks once they fledge.

Left: The herring gull's pink legs are a distinctive feature.

Identification: White head and underparts, with grey on the back and wings. Prominent large, white spots on the black flight feathers. Distinctive pink feet. Reddish spot towards the tip of the lower bill. Some dark streaking on the head and neck in winter. Sexes alike. The young birds are mainly brown, with prominent barring on their wings and dark bills.

Distribution: Atlantic, north of Iceland and south to northern coast of Spain, through the North Sea and Baltic areas, north of Scandinavia.
Size: 60cm (24in)
Habitat: Coastal and inland areas.
Nest: Small pile of vegetation.
Eggs: 2–3, pale blue to brown with darker markings.
Food: Fish and carrion.

Black-headed gull

Larus ridibundus

These gulls are a common sight not only in coastal areas but also in town parks with lakes. They move inland during the winter. They are also often seen following tractors ploughing at this time of year, seeking worms and grubs in the soil. Black-headed gulls nest close to water in what can be quite large colonies. Like many gulls, they are noisy birds, even calling at night. On warm, summer evenings, they can sometimes be seen hawking flying ants and similar insects in flight, demonstrating their airborne agility.

Identification: These gulls have their distinctive black heads only during the summer, with a white collar beneath and white underparts. Wings are grey, and the flight feathers mainly black. In the winter, the head is mainly white, aside from black ear coverts, and a black smudge above each eye. In the winter, the bill is red at the base and dark at the tip.

Distribution: Across most of Europe into Asia. Also present on the North African side of the Mediterranean.
Size: 39cm (15in).
Habitat: Coastal areas.
Nest: Scrape lined with plant matter.
Eggs: 2–3, pale blue to brown with darker markings.
Food: Typically molluscs, crustaceans and small fish.

Above: The black feathering on the head is a transient characteristic, appearing only in the summer (above right).

Great black-backed gull

Larus marinus

These large gulls can be extremely disruptive when close to nesting seabird colonies. Not only will they harry returning birds for their catches of fish, but they also take eggs and chicks on occasion too. In winter, great black-backed gulls move inland to scavenge on rubbish tips, although they are generally wary of people and are unlikely to be seen in urban areas. Banding studies have revealed that many of those that overwinter in Britain are actually birds of Norwegian origin, which return to Scandinavia to breed the following spring. Pairs are often quite solitary at this time, especially when nesting near people, but they are more likely to nest in colonies on uninhabited islands.

Identification: Has a white head and underparts with black on the back and wings. Is a large size. Has a white-spotted black tail and a large area of white is apparent at the wing tips in flight. The bill is yellow with red tip to the lower bill. Has pale pinkish legs. Sexes alike.

Distribution: From northern Spain north to Iceland and eastwards through the North Sea and Baltic to Scandinavia. Also present on the eastern side of North America.
Size: 74cm (29in).
Habitat: Coastal areas.
Nest: Pile of vegetation.
Eggs: 2–3, brownish with dark markings.
Food: Fish and carrion.

Lesser black-backed gull (*Larus fuscus*): 56cm (22in)
Breeds around the shores of the extreme north of Europe, moving as far south as parts of North Africa in the winter. Similar to the great black-backed but smaller and lacks the prominent white seen on the flight feathers when the wings are closed. Legs are yellow rather than dull pink. Much smaller area of white on the outstretched upper surface of the wings in flight. Sexes alike.

Kittiwake (*Larus tridactyla*): 42cm (17in)
Occurs widely around the shores of northern Europe, down to the western Mediterranean. White head and underparts, with grey on the back and wings. Yellow bill, dark feet and black flight feathers. In winter plumage, grey extends to the back of the head, with blackish, crescent-shaped marking behind the eyes. Sexes alike. Young birds have more black on the wings and a black collar.

Glaucous gull (*Larus hyperboreus*): 68cm (27in)
Coastal areas of northern Europe, including Iceland. Very pale bluish-grey wings with white edges. Head and underparts white in summer, developing grey streaks in winter. Sexes alike. As in other species, young birds are more mottled overall.

Yellow-legged gull (*Larus cachinnans*): 58cm (23in)
Found in coastal areas of southern England and mainland Europe to North Africa, and also around the Black and Caspian seas. Has a white head and underparts, grey back and wings and small white spots on the black flight feathers. The wings have large black areas towards the tips. The bill and legs are yellow and there is a red spot on the lower bill. Grey suffusion on the head in winter. Sexes alike. Was recognized as a form of the herring gull (*L. argentatus*) but now considered a separate species.

Common gull

Larus canus

The common gulls often ranges over considerable distances inland, seeking earthworms and other invertebrates to feed on. In sandy coastal areas they will search for shellfish as well. There is a distinct seasonal variation in the range of these gulls. They leave their breeding grounds in Scandinavia and Russia at the end of the summer, heading further south in Europe to France and various locations in the Mediterranean. They overwinter here before migrating north again in the spring. In spite of its rather meek appearance, this species will bully smaller gulls such as the black-headed gull to take food from them. Common gulls and black-headed gulls are often found in the same type of environment inland and tend to show a preference for grassland and agricultural areas.

Distribution: Iceland, Great Britain and the Baltic region. Main breeding grounds are in Scandinavia and Russia. Extends across Asia to western North America.
Size: 46cm (18in).
Habitat: Coasts and inland areas close to water.
Nest: Raised nest of twigs and other debris.
Eggs: 2–3, pale blue to brownish olive with dark markings.
Food: Shellfish, small fish and invertebrates.

Identification: White head and underparts with yellow bill and yellowish-green legs. Wings are greyish with white markings at the tips, which are most visible in flight. Flight feathers are black with white spots. Tail is white. Dark eyes. Greyish streaking on the head in winter plumage. Sexes alike. Young birds have brown mottled plumage and it takes them more than two years to obtain adult coloration.

TERNS

Terns as a group can usually be distinguished quite easily, even from gulls, by their relatively elongated shape. Their long, pointed wings are an indication of their aerial ability, and some terns regularly fly longer distances than other migrants. Not surprisingly, their flight appears to be almost effortless. When breeding, terns tend to nest in colonies.

Common tern

Sterna hirundo

These terns are only likely to be encountered in northern parts of their range between April and October, after which they head south to warmer climes for the duration of the winter. Travelling long distances means that they are powerful in flight and yet are also agile. Their strongly forked tail helps them to hover effectively, adjusting their position before diving in search of fish. Their long bills provide another simple way of distinguishing them from gulls. This species is represented on all continents and is very versatile in its feeding habits. Common terns may hawk food on the wing or dive into the oceans to obtain their quarry.

Identification: Long body shape with black on the top of the head extending down the back of the neck. Rest of the face and underparts whitish grey. Back and wings greyish, with long flight feathers. Narrow white streamers on the tail. Bill red, aside from the dark tip, which becomes completely black in the winter. The plumage in front of the eyes becomes white during this time. Legs and feet red. Sexes alike.

Distribution: Great Britain and Scandinavia and much of Central Europe during the summer, migrating south to parts of western and southern Africa for the winter.
Size: 36cm (14in).
Habitat: Near water.
Nest: Scrape on the ground.
Eggs: 3, pale brown with dark spots.
Food: Mainly fish, but also eats crustaceans.

Sandwich tern

Cabot's tern *Sterna sandvicensis*

A summer visitor to northern Europe, this species is often sighted slightly earlier than the common tern and then leaves just before its relative. The sandwich tern is significantly larger, and also surprisingly noisy, with the sounds of its calls having been likened to those of a grating cartwheel. Although these terns may skim over the water surface seeking food, they also dive spectacularly from heights of as much as 10m (33ft). Sandwich terns usually breed in high-density colonies in the open on sand bars and similarly exposed coastal sites, although they may sometimes nest on islands in lakes.

Identification: Shaggy black crest evident at the back of the head. The entire top of the head is black during the summer, while a white forehead is characteristic of the winter plumage. The bill is long and black with a yellow tip. Rest of the head and underparts are white, and the wings are grey. Sexes alike.

Distribution: Found around the shores of Great Britain and northern Europe, as well as the Caspian and Black seas, wintering further south in the Mediterranean region and Africa. Also occurs in parts of southern Asia, the Caribbean and South America.
Size: 43cm (17in).
Habitat: Coastal areas.
Nest: Scrape on the ground.
Eggs: 1–2, brownish white with darker markings.
Food: Fish, especially sand eels.

Roseate tern

Sterna dougallii

In northern parts of their range, these terns are brief summer visitors, only likely to be present from about the middle of May until the end of August. Their distribution is quite localized. They are most likely to be seen where the shore is shallow and sandy, providing them with better fishing opportunities. They dive into the water to catch their prey from heights of no more than 2m (7ft). They may also take fish from other terns, and their shorter wings and quicker wing beats make them more agile in flight. Unlike some other terns, roseate terns avoid open areas when nesting, preferring sites concealed among rocks or vegetation.

Identification: This tern gets its name from the slight pinkish suffusion on its whitish underparts. Compared to other terns, has relatively long tail streamers and quite short wings. The bill is primarily blackish with a red base in the summer. The entire top of the head is black in the summer, and the forehead becomes white in winter. Sexes alike. Subspecies differ in both wing and bill length.

Distribution: The British Isles south to Spain and North Africa. Winters in western Africa.
Size: 36cm (14in).
Habitat: Coastal areas.
Nest: Scrape on the ground.
Eggs: 1–2, cream or buff eggs with reddish-brown markings.
Food: Mainly fish.

Little tern (*Sterna albifrons*): 25cm (10in)
Found in coastal areas in northern Europe. Also breeds in central Europe. Overwinters in Africa. Has a white forehead with black edges. These form a black cap that extends down the nape of the neck. The bill is yellow with a black tip. The legs are orange-yellow. Has black edges to the primary feathers, while the remainder of the wings are grey. The chest and underparts are white. Sexes are alike.

Caspian tern (*Sterna caspia*): 55cm (22in)
Breeds mainly in the Baltic region, overwintering in western Africa. Is sometimes seen in the Mediterranean area. Has a black top to the head that becomes streaked in winter plumage. Has grey wings and a white chest and underparts. Large red bill with black tip. Sexes are alike.

Lesser crested tern (*Sterna bengalensis*):
40cm (16in)
Found along the North African coast and less commonly in the Gulf of Suez and the Red Sea. Occasionally seen in Europe. Black top to the head with a crest. Wings, rump and upper tail are grey. Remainder of the plumage is white. Has a slender yellow bill. The legs are black. In winter plumage, the area of black on the head is reduced. Sexes are alike.

Gull-billed tern (*Sterna nilotica*):
42cm (17in)
Ranges from the coast of northern mainland Europe south to the Mediterranean. Winters in Africa. Black cap on the head extends down to the nape of the neck. Frosty grey wings, back and tail feathers, which have white edges. Remainder of the plumage is white. In winter plumage, the black cap is replaced by blackish ear coverts. Bill relatively short and black. Sexes are alike.

Arctic tern

Sterna paradisaea

It can be very difficult to distinguish this species from the common tern, but the Arctic tern's bill is shorter and does not have a black tip in the summer. The tail, too, is longer, and the tail streamers are very evident in flight. Arctic terns undertake the most extensive migrations of any birds, flying almost from one end of the world to the other. Breeding in the vicinity of the Arctic Circle, these birds then head south, often beyond Africa to Antarctica, before repeating the journey the following year, although it appears that at least some young birds stay for their first full year in the Antarctic Ocean. Arctic terns will nest communally, often frequenting islands for breeding purposes. They react aggressively to a potential predator in their midst, with a number of individuals turning on and mobbing any intruder. Arctic terns may steal food from other birds – for example, from puffins in the Faeroe Islands.

Identification: Black area covering the entire top of the head, with white chest and underparts. Wings grey. Bill dark red, becoming black in the winter when the forehead is white. Sexes alike.

Distribution: Breeds in northern Europe and the Arctic, overwintering in southern Africa.
Size: 38cm (15in).
Habitat: Seas and fresh water.
Nest: Hollow on the ground, lined with vegetation.
Eggs: 2, brownish, bluish or greenish with dark markings.
Food: Fish and invertebrates.

WADERS

The description of 'wader' is given to birds that usually inhabit shallow waters, seeking their food as they walk along an uncovered beach or mudflat at low tide. Waders are often sighted in mixed groups, taking advantage of feeding opportunities as these become available. Seasonal movements of waders are quite common, with some breeding in the far north during the summer months

Eurasian oystercatcher

Haematopus ostralegus

The large size of these waders, coupled with their noisy nature, makes them quite conspicuous. The oystercatcher's powerful bill is a surprisingly adaptable tool, allowing these birds not only to force mussel shells apart, but also to hammer limpets off groynes and even prey on crabs. Inland, oystercatchers use their bills to catch earthworms in the soil without difficulty. Individuals will defend favoured feeding sites such as mussel beds from others of their own kind, although oystercatchers may sometimes form large flocks of thousands of individuals, especially in the winter.

Identification: The head, upper chest and wings are black. The underparts are white and there is a white stripe on the wings. Has a prominent, straight orangish-red bill, which may be shorter and thicker in cock birds. Legs are reddish. In winter plumage, adults have a white throat and collar and pale pink legs. Sexes are alike.

Distribution: Around the shores of Europe, especially Great Britain, extending to Asia. Also present in North Africa.
Size: 44cm (17in.)
Habitat: Tidal mudflats, sometimes in fields.
Nest: Scrape on the ground.
Eggs: 2–4, light buff with blackish-brown markings.
Food: Cockles, mussels and similar prey.

Avocet

Pied avocet *Recurvirostra avosetta*

The unique shape of the avocet's long, thin, upward-curving bill enables these birds to feed by sweeping the bill from side to side in the water, locating their prey predominantly by touch. Pairs may show very aggressive behaviour when breeding. They can be present in large numbers, nesting at high densities, in some areas. Although they most frequently move about by wading, avocets can also swim well and will place their heads under water when seeking food. When migrating, avocets tend to fly quite low in loose lines. Birds from western areas tend to be more sedentary compared with those occurring further east. These tend to overwinter in Africa as well as the Mediterranean region.

Identification: Slender, with long, pale blue legs. The black plumage on the top of the head extends down to the nape. Black stripes extend over the shoulder area and around the sides of the wings. Black flight feathers. Long, thin black bill curves upwards at the tip. Hens often have shorter bills and a brownish tinge to their black markings.

Distribution: North-western Europe, often close to the coast, and southern Europe and North Africa. Also extends into western Asia.
Size: 46cm (18in.)
Habitat: Lagoons and mudflats.
Nest: Scrape on the ground lined with vegetation.
Eggs: 4, pale brown with faint markings.
Food: Small crustaceans and other invertebrates.

Black-winged stilt (*Himantopus himantopus*):
36cm (14in)
Found in southern Europe. Overwinters in Africa.
The top of the head to the nape is blackish. The
ear coverts are black. The back and wings are jet
black and the underparts are white. The bill is
long and black. The legs are very long and red.
Sexes are similar, except that hens lack the dark
head markings and the plumage on the back is
more brownish in colour.

Sanderling (*Calidris alba*): 20cm (8in)
Breeds in the Arctic. Can be seen on migration
and during the winter on the shores of Europe.
Has a rufous coloration and black speckling on the
breast. The underparts are white. The back and
wings are grey with black and buff markings.
During the winter, rufous markings are less
evident but a broad wing bar with black edging is
seen in flight. Sexes are alike.

Knot (*Calidris canutus*): 25cm (10in)
Breeds in the Arctic and migrates south along
northern and western European coasts as far
as North Africa. Distinctive rufous underparts in
summer, with black and rufous speckling on the
wings offset against areas of grey plumage. Black
legs and grey upperparts. In winter plumage has
streaking on the head, chest and flanks, greyish-
white underparts and grey-green legs. Sexes alike.

Dunlin (red-backed sandpiper, *Calidris alpina*):
20cm (8in)
Circumpolar. Greyish head and wings in winter
plumage with streaking on the breast.
Underparts are white. In summer, has a more
distinctive black streaking, with brownish and
black plumage on the wings. The abdomen is
mainly black. Has white flanks. Sexes are alike.

Stone curlew

Thick knee *Burhinus oedicnemus*

The stone curlew is a wader that has
adapted to a relatively dry environment,
and its mottled plumage enables it to blend
in well against a stony background. When
frightened, it drops to the ground in an
attempt to conceal its presence. These birds
are also frequently active after dark, when
they will be much harder to observe. Their
loud call notes may be heard, however,
sounding rather like "curlee" and audible
over distances of 2.5km (1.5m)
when the surroundings are
quiet. On occasion, stone
curlews living close to coastal
areas fly to mudflats, feeding
when the flats are exposed
by the sea.

Distribution: Breeds at
various localities in Europe,
extending from southern
England southwards. Ranges
into southern Asia and south
to parts of northern Africa.
Size: 45cm (18in).
Habitat: Open, relatively dry
countryside.
Nest: Bare scrape on
the ground.
Eggs: 2, pale buff with
dark markings.
Food: Invertebrates, typically
caught at night.

Identification: Streaked plumage
on the neck, upper breast and
wings, with prominent white
stripes above and below the
eyes. White wing bars edged
with black are also apparent on
the wings. Abdomen and
throat are whitish. Long,
thick yellowish legs. Bill is
mainly blackish, but yellow at
the base. Sexes alike. However,
there is a little variation among
races and some have a greyer
tint to their feathers than others.

Ringed plover

Greater ringed plover *Charadrius hiaticula*

In spite of their relatively small size,
these waders have strong migratory
instincts. They breed mainly
in the far north, and are
most likely to be seen in
Europe during May and
again from the middle of
August for about a month.
After that time, they leave
European shores on their way
south to Africa for the winter.
Ringed plovers typically breed
on beaches and on the tundra.
They can be seen in reasonably
large flocks outside the nesting
season, often seeking food in
tidal areas.

Identification: Black mask extends over the
forehead and down across the eyes. There is a
white patch above the bill and just behind the
eyes. A broad black band extends across the chest.
The underparts are otherwise white. The wings
are a greyish brown and the bill is orange with
a black tip. In winter plumage, the black areas
are reduced, apart from the bill which
becomes entirely blackish.
White areas extend
from the forehead
to above the eyes.
Cheek patches are
greyish brown and there
is a similar band on the upper chest
at this time. Sexes are alike.

Distribution: Western
Europe and North America,
wintering in Africa. Also
recorded in parts of Asia.
Size: 19cm (7.5in).
Habitat: Coastal areas and
tundra.
Nest: Bare scrape on the
ground.
Eggs: 4, stone-buff with
black markings.
Food: Freshwater and marine
invertebrates.

WATERBIRDS

Although some waterbirds, such as herons, feed in a similar fashion to waders, their larger size allows them to wander into deeper water, and thus affords them greater opportunity to feed, as well as enabling them to take larger prey such as fish. Certain waterbirds such as divers will actually disappear under the water in search of food, however, rather than hunting from above.

Grey heron

Ardea cinerea

These large, opportunistic hunters are often shy on the ground and can be hard to spot. They are usually seen in flight, with their long necks tucked back on to their shoulders and their legs held out behind the body. They fly with relatively slow, quite noisy wing beats. When hunting, grey herons are patient predators. They stand motionless, looking closely for any sign of movement in the water around them, lunging quickly with their powerful bills to grab any fish or frog that swims within reach. During the winter, when their freshwater habitats are frozen, grey herons often move to river estuaries in search of food. These birds frequently nest in colonies, with some breeding sites being used for centuries by successive generations.

Identification: Powerful yellow bill. White head with black area and longer plumes off the back of the head. Long neck and chest are whitish with a black stripe running down the centre. Wings are grey with black areas at the shoulder. Underparts are lighter grey. Long yellowish legs. Sexes alike.

Distribution: Throughout most of Europe into Asia, apart from the far north. Also occurs in North Africa and ranges south around the Sahara Desert.
Size: 100cm (39in).
Habitat: Areas of water with reeds.
Nest: Platform of sticks built off the ground.
Eggs: 3–5, chalky blue.
Food: Fish and other aquatic vertebrates.

Eurasian spoonbill

Platalea leucorodia

Distribution: Breeds in northern temperate parts of Europe and Asia, as far east as China. Winters further south in tropical parts of Africa and South-east Asia. Indian birds are sedentary.
Size: 93cm (37in).
Habitat: Mudflats and marshes.
Nest: Stick platforms off the ground.
Eggs: 3–4, white with brown markings.
Food: Fish, other aquatic creatures and vegetation.

The enlarged surface area of these birds' bills enables them to feed more easily as they move their heads from side to side in the water. Young spoonbills, however, have a narrower, light-coloured bill with no enlargement at its tip. They can also be identified in flight by the black tips to their outer flight feathers. It can take up to four years for them to start nesting, and they may live for nearly 30 years. Spoonbills can swim if they need to, but they usually inhabit calm, shallow stretches of water. When resting, they may perch on one leg and tuck their bills over their backs. In flight, however, they will extend their necks.

Identification: Highly distinctive enlarged, yellow-edged, spoon-like tip to the black bill. Has a crest of feathers on the back of the neck that is longer in the male, and an orange patch of plumage on the chest at breeding time. The rest of the feathering is white. The legs are black.

White stork

Ciconia ciconia

Distribution: Summer visitor to much of mainland Europe. Winters in western and eastern parts of North Africa, depending on the flight path. Also occurs in Asia.
Size: 110cm (43in).
Habitat: Wetland areas.
Nest: Large platform of sticks, located off the ground.
Eggs: 3–5, chalky white.
Food: Amphibians, fish, small mammals and invertebrates.

Considered to be a harbinger of good fortune, these birds often return year after year to the same nest site on the top of a building, adding annually to their nest, which can develop into a bulky structure. The return of these storks in the spring from their wintering grounds in Africa helped to foster the widespread myth of the link between storks and babies. The migration of white storks on their two flight paths in April each year – over the Strait of Gibraltar and further east over the Bosphorus – is a spectacular sight. They fly with their long necks extended and their legs trailing behind their bodies. The journey back to Africa is repeated each August. The numbers of white storks have declined in some areas over recent years due to drainage of their wetland habitat.

Identification: Large, tall, mainly white bird with prominent black areas on the back and wings. Has a long red bill and legs. Sexes are alike. Young birds are smaller and have a dark tip to the bill.

Great crested grebe

Podiceps cristatus

Great crested grebes are primarily aquatic birds and their flying ability is restricted by their short wings. They can dive very effectively, however, and often disappear underwater if they feel threatened. Rarely observed on land, these grebes are relatively cumbersome because their legs are located well back on the body and this restricts their ability to move fast across open ground. Their toes are not fully webbed, unlike those of waterfowl, but they can swim quickly thanks to the stream-lined shape of their body. They use the ruff-type facial feathers during their display.

Distribution: Europe east to China and southwards across much of Africa. Also Australia and New Zealand.
Size: 51cm (20in).
Habitat: Extensive reedy stretches of water.
Nest: Mound of reeds.
Eggs: 3–6, chalky white.
Food: Fish and invertebrates.

Identification: Black from top of the head down to the back. Brownish areas on sides of body in winter. During summer, there is an extensive black crest, with a chestnut ruff at rear of head edged with black. Bill reddish pink. Sexes alike.

Great northern loon (common loon, *Gavia immer*): 88cm (35in)
Present on Icelandic and British coasts. Also occurs in North America and Greenland. Has a black head, with barring on the neck and throat. The back is patterned black and white and has white spots. The underparts are white. There is less contrast in the winter plumage, with white extending from the lower bill and throat down over the underparts. In winter, the eyes are dark rather than red. Sexes are alike.

Little grebe (*Tachybaptus ruficollis*): 29cm (11in)
Found in most of Europe on a line from southern Scotland southwards. Also present in North Africa and the Middle East. Black head, chestnut patches on the neck and a yellow gape at the corners of the bill. Dark feathering on the back and wings with brown flanks. In the winter, light buff plumage replaces darker areas. Sexes alike.

Little egret (*Egretta garzetta*): 65cm (26in)
Southern Europe, overwintering mainly in Africa and the Middle East. White plumage, with blue-grey area at the base of the bill. Long, white nuptial plumes at breeding time. Legs blackish, but with very unusual yellow toes. Sexes alike.

CRAKES

This group of birds may be observed in the open, but, if frightened, they usually dart back into cover along the edges of the stretches of water that they usually frequent. They can all be recognized by their relatively narrow body shape, which enables them to slip easily and quietly through reeds and similar vegetation.

Water rail

Rallus aquaticus

Being naturally highly adaptable, these rails have an extensive distribution, and have even been recorded foraging in tidal areas surrounded by seaweed in the Scilly Isles off south-west England. In some parts of their range, they migrate to warmer climes for the winter. Water rails survive in Iceland during the winter thanks to the hot thermal springs, which never freeze. Water rails are very territorial when breeding and, as in other related species, their chicks hatch in a precocial state.

Identification: Prominent, long, reddish bill with bluish-grey breast and sides to the head. Narrow, brownish line extending over the top of the head down the back and wings, which have black markings. Black-and-white barring on the flanks and underparts. Short tail with pale buff underparts. Sexes alike.

Distribution: Extensive, from Iceland throughout most of Europe, south to North Africa and east across Asia to Siberia, China and Japan.
Size: 26cm (10in).
Habitat: Reed beds and sedge.
Nest: Cup made of vegetation.
Eggs: 5–16, whitish with reddish-brown spotting.
Food: Mainly animal matter, but also some vegetation.

Coot

Eurasian coot *Fulica atra*

Open stretches of water are important to coots, enabling them to dive in search of food. During the winter, these birds may sometimes assemble in flocks on larger stretches of waters that are unlikely to freeze over at this time. These coots may find food on land or in the water, although they dive only briefly in relatively shallow water. When breeding, pairs are very territorial, attacking chicks of other coots that venture too close, and even their own chicks, which they grab by the neck. Such behaviour is often described as tousling. The young usually respond by feigning death and this results in them being left alone.

Identification: Has a sooty, grey, plump body with a black neck and head. The bill is white with a white frontal plate. This iris is a dark brownish colour. A white trailing edge on the wings is evident in flight. Long toes have no webbing. Sexes are alike.

Distribution: From Great Britain east throughout Europe, except the far north, south into North Africa and east to Asia, as well as Australia and New Zealand.
Size: 42cm (16.5in.)
Habitat: Still and slow-flowing stretches of water.
Nest: Pile of reeds at the water's edge.
Eggs: 1–14, buff to brown with dark markings.
Food: Plant and animal matter.

Spotted crake (*Porzana porzana*): 22cm (9in)
Found in western and central parts of Eurasia and as far east as southern Siberia and north-west China. Winters in North Africa and south-wards from Ethiopia . Has a distinctive, heavily white-spotted breast, although the abdomen is streakier. Has prominent brown ear coverts, with a bluish-grey stripe above, and black markings on the wings. The undertail area is pale buff and whiter at the tip, but may show dark spots in some cases. The bill is yellow, although red at the base. Sexes are alike.

Little crake (*Porzana parva*): 19cm (7.5in)
Found in areas of Spain and Portugal. The range then extends eastwards through Europe to China. Overwinters in southern Asia and northern parts of Africa. Has a slaty-blue head and underparts. Black markings are found predominantly across the top of the wings. The remainder of the back is brown. Has a black-and-white speckled under-tail area. The bill is yellow with a red base. Adult hens are easily distinguished by their white chest area which turns buff on the underparts. Sexes are alike.

Baillon's crake (*Porzana pusilla*): 18cm (7in)
Has a sporadic distribution through Europe and overwinters in North Africa. Also occurs further south, in Africa and on Madagascar. Ranges through Asia to parts of Australia and New Zealand. Has a slaty-blue head and underparts, although the Baillon's crake can be distinguished from the little crake by far more extensive barring on the flanks and heavier white speckling on the wings. The bill is dull with no red area. Hens may have paler plumage on the throat.

Moorhen

Common moorhen *Gallinula chloropus*

Although usually found in areas of fresh water, moorhens are occasionally seen in brackish areas – for example, on the Namibian coast in south-western Africa. Their long toes enable them to walk over aquatic vegetation, and they also feed when swimming or browsing on land. Their diet varies according to the season, although seeds of various types make up the bulk of their food. If danger threatens, moorhens will either dive or swim underwater. They are adept divers, remaining submerged by grasping on to underwater vegetation with their bills. In public parks, moorhens can become quite tame, darting in to obtain food provided for ducks.

Identification: Slate-grey head, back and underparts. Greyish-black wings. A prominent white line runs down the sides of the body. The area under the tail is white and has a black central stripe. Greenish-yellow legs have a small red area at the top. The bill is red apart from a yellow tip. Sexes are alike.

Distribution: Very wide, from Great Britain east throughout Europe except for the far north. Occurs through much of Africa, especially southern parts, and also through much of South-east Asia and parts of the Americas.
Size: 30cm (12in).
Habitat: Ponds and other areas of water edged by dense vegetation.
Nest: Domed structure hidden in reeds.
Eggs: 2–17, buff to light green with dark markings.
Food: Omnivorous.

Purple swamp hen

Porphyrio porphyrio

The European population of the purple swamp hen has become much scarcer over recent years because of habitat changes, specifically drainage of the wetland areas. In some other localities, however, such as the Nile Valley of Egypt, the species has expanded its range thanks to the greater availability of suitable habitat created by irrigation schemes. Purple swamp hens are most likely to be observed late in the day, when they venture out in search of food. These birds are rather clumsy on short flights, literally running across the surface of the water to take off, and flying with their legs hanging down rather than being held against the body. They are unable to fly when moulting.

Identification: Relatively large, with vivid blue and purplish shades predominating in the plumage and prominent white undertail coverts. The wings especially may have a greenish hue in some cases. Bill is dull red with brighter frontal plate. Long legs are pinkish red. Sexes alike.

Distribution: Southern Europe, sporadic locations in North Africa and southern parts of that continent. Also present in Asia, Australia and New Zealand.
Size: 50cm (20in).
Habitat: Reedy lakes and marshes.
Nest: Platform of vegetation just above the water.
Eggs: 2–7, whitish to green with dark spots.
Food: Mostly vegetarian.

WETLAND BIRDS

These birds can be encountered in a range of habitats, typically close to coastal areas. In many cases, their plumage provides them with excellent camouflage, allowing them to blend in against the background. They have relatively long legs and an upright stance, as well as a bill that enables them to seek food in shallow water.

Curlew

Eurasian curlew *Numenius arquata*

The distinctive call note of the curlew, which gives it its name, is audible from some distance away. This wader's large size and its long, narrow bill also help to identify it. Its legs are so long that its toes protrude beyond the tip of the tail when in flight. Curlews are most likely to be observed in coastal areas outside the breeding season. They feed here by probing in the sand with their bills, although elsewhere they use their bills to pick berries and catch snails.

Left: Curlews return to the same wintering grounds each year, and can live for more than 30 years.

Identification: Streaked plumage, with lighter ground colour on the throat and buff chest. Larger dark patterning on the wings. Underparts and rump are white. Cocks have plain-coloured heads, but hens' heads usually show a trace of a white stripe running down over the crown. Hens can also be distinguished by their longer bills, up to 15cm (6in) long. Grey rather than buff plumage when not breeding.

Distribution: Present throughout the year in the British Isles and adjacent areas of northern Europe. Also breeds widely elsewhere in Europe and Asia, migrating south to the Mediterranean and Africa in winter.
Size: 57cm (22in).
Habitat: Marshland, moorland and coastal areas.
Nest: Scrape on the ground concealed by vegetation.
Eggs: 4, greenish brown with darker spots.
Food: Omnivorous.

Little ringed plover

Charadrius dubius

These plovers favour areas with exposed gravel for breeding purposes, and their coloration helps to camouflage them very effectively. Little ringed plovers migrate from their breeding grounds in Europe typically by the end of September, and return the following March. They are more likely to be seen in coastal regions outside the breeding period. They do not tend to associate in mixed flocks with other waders, choosing instead to form small groups on their own. These birds may also be seen near temporarily flooded areas on occasion, including farmland.

Identification: Broad black lines extend across the top of the forehead and from the bill back around the eye. A broader black band runs across the chest. The brown crown is surrounded by white, which also forms a collar around the neck. The entire underparts are white and the legs are pinkish brown. The bill is black. In winter plumage, the entire head is brownish, with a pale buff area above the bill extending above the eyes. Chest collar is a brownish grey rather than black. The sexes are alike.

Distribution: Ranges from southern Scandinavia south across much of Europe, wintering in Africa. Also present in Asia.
Size: 18cm (7in).
Habitat: Sandy areas near fresh water.
Nest: Scrape on the ground.
Eggs: 3, stone-buff with dark markings.
Food: Invertebrates.

Red-wattled lapwing (*Vanellus indicus*):
35cm (14in)
Found in south-eastern Turkey, the Middle East and southern Asia. Has black feathering on the head. White areas on the sides of the face extend down around the black breast and on to the underparts and rump. The back and wings are brown. The bill and an area around the eyes are red. The legs are yellow. The black flight feathers and a band across the tail are evident in flight. Sexes are alike.

Pacific golden plover (*Pluvialis fulva*):
25cm (10in)
Breeds in the far north of Europe, including Iceland, and may winter as far south as North Africa. Black area on the sides of the face extends down over the chest and underparts, which is bordered by white feathering and barring from above the bill down the sides of the body. Coarse, mottled pattern of brown, black and white plumage over the wings. Very upright stance on grey legs. In winter plumage underparts also become mottled with black-and-white feathering. Sexes alike.

Black-winged pratincole (*Glareola nordmanni*):
28cm (11in)
Ranges from the eastern Mediterranean north into Asia in summer and overwinters largely in southern Africa. Has a black area on the forehead and lores extending down to form a stripe under the bill and there is a buff-coloured area under the throat. The remainder of the plumage is brownish grey with white underparts. The bill is dull with little red apparent, and becomes even blacker during the winter. The contrast in the plumage at this time is also reduced. Sexes alike.

Lapwing

Northern lapwing *Vanellus vanellus*

These birds are also known as peewits in some areas because of the sound of their calls. Flocks of lapwings are a common sight in farmland areas where they comb the ploughed soil for invertebrates. They are quite easily recognized from a distance because of their crests. Lapwings may breed in loose groups, and the scrape that is used by a pair is lined with what often becomes quite a substantial pile of vegetation. The lapwing may move long distances during prolonged spells of severe winter weather, sometimes congregating in huge flocks in estuaries when freshwater areas become frozen.

Distribution: Occurs from southern Scandinavia southwards to the Mediterranean, and migrates eastwards as far as Japan. Also occurs in North Africa and may also be seen further south.
Size: 30cm (12in).
Habitat: Marshland and farmland.
Nest: Scrape on the ground.
Eggs: 4, light brown with dark markings.
Food: Mainly invertebrates.

Identification: Long, narrow, black backward-curving crest, with black on the face, which is separated by a white streak in hens. Underparts are white, apart from chestnut undertail coverts. Wings are dark green, with a greyer-green area on the neck. The white cheek patches behind the eyes are broken by a black line. Outside the breeding period, the facial plumage is buff, and white areas are restricted to the chin and throat.

Snipe

Common snipe *Gallinago gallinago*

These waders are very shy by nature, and may even be nocturnal in their feeding habits, probing damp ground with jerky movements of their stocky bills. If surprised in the open, snipes sometimes freeze but often they take off almost vertically, powering away and flying in a zigzag fashion, before plunging back down into suitable cover. In some parts of their range, such as the British Isles, they remain sedentary. Those inhabiting more northerly latitudes, however, often migrate south to Africa to avoid severe winter weather, when frozen ground makes it difficult for them to find sufficient food.

Identification: Pale buff stripe running down the centre of the crown, with buff stripes above and below the eyes. Dark mottled plumage on the chest and wings. Underparts are white. White stripes run down the wing, with a white border to the rear of the wings. Long bill, which may be larger in hens. Sexes otherwise alike.

Distribution: Ranges from Iceland both west across North America and east through Europe and Asia. May migrate to southerly latitudes for the winter.
Size: 28cm (11in).
Habitat: Marshland and wet pasture.
Nest: Scrape on the ground.
Eggs: 3, greenish buff with dark markings.
Food: Invertebrates.

SWANS AND GEESE

These large, unmistakable birds regularly fly long distances to and from their breeding grounds, especially swans. They also rank among the longest-lived of all waterfowl, with a possible life expectancy of more than two decades. Young birds are unlikely to breed until they are three or four years old. When observing them, remember that both geese and swans can be aggressive on occasion.

Mute swan

Cygnus olor

These swans are seen in a wide range of habitats, and may even venture on to the sea occasionally, although they do not stray far from the shore. They prefer to feed on aquatic vegetation, but will sometimes graze on short grass. In town and city parks, mute swans often eat a greater variety of foods, such as grain and bread provided for them. They rarely dive, but use their long necks to dabble under the surface of the water to obtain food. Pairs are very territorial when breeding, and the male swan, called the cob, will actively try to drive away people who venture too close with fierce movements of its wings.

Identification: Mainly white, with a black area extending from the eyes to the base of the orange bill. A swollen knob protrudes over the upper part of the bill. The legs and feet are blackish. Hens are smaller with a less pronounced knob on the bill. Traces of staining are often evident on the head and neck. Young birds are browner.

Distribution: Resident in the British Isles and adjacent areas of western Europe, often living in a semi-domesticated state. Also occurs in parts of Asia. Localized introduced populations in South Africa, the eastern USA, Australia and New Zealand.
Size: 160cm (63in).
Habitat: Larger stretches of fresh water and estuaries.
Nest: Large pile of heaped-up aquatic vegetation.
Eggs: 5–7, pale green.
Food: Mainly vegetation.

Whooper swan

Cygnus cygnus

Although some Icelandic whooper swans are sedentary throughout the year, the majority of these birds undertake regular migrations, so they are likely to be observed in southern Europe only during the winter months. They often frequent areas around inland waterways at this time, such as the Black and Caspian seas. Pairs nest on their own, and the young chicks fly alongside their parents on the journey south. In the winter, whooper swans may sometimes invade agricultural areas, where they eat a wide range of foods varying from potatoes to acorns, although generally they prefer to feed on aquatic vegetation.

Identification: Body plumage is white, although it may sometimes be stained. The base of the bill is yellow, extending as far down as the nostrils, and the tip is black. Legs and feet are grey. Hens are a little smaller, while young birds have pinkish rather than yellow bases to their bills.

Above left: These swans fly in a V-shaped formation when migrating. Huge numbers may congregate together at their wintering grounds.

Distribution: Iceland and Scandinavia east to Siberia. Overwinters further south.
Size: 165cm (65in).
Habitat: Ponds and lakes, typically in wooded areas. Often overwinters close to the coast.
Nest: Mounds of plant matter, often moss.
Eggs: 3–7, pale green.
Food: Vegetation.

Berwick's swan (tundra swan, *Cygnus columbianus*): 127cm (50in)
Present on the Northern coast of the Americas and migrates south for the winter. Also present on the northern Russian coast to Siberia and winters in the British Isles and north-western Europe. Overwinters south of the Caspian Sea and at a similar latitude in eastern Asia. White, with yellow on the bill that never extends to the nostrils. Hen is smaller in size.

Pink-footed goose (*Anser brachyrhynchus*): 75cm (29.5in)
Found in eastern Greenland, Iceland and Spitzbergen. Overwinters in northern Britain and Denmark southwards. Has a brown head with white streaking on the neck and more prominent markings on the wings and underparts. Bill is pinkish but dark at its base. Legs and feet are pinkish. Sexes alike.

Barnacle goose (*Branta leucopsis*): 70cm (27.5in)
Found in eastern Greenland, Spitzbergen, Novaya Zemlya and Baltic areas. Winters in the British Isles and north-western Europe. Black line from the bill to the eyes. Facial area is mainly white. Neck and upper breast are black. Whitish underparts with grey barring. Wings are grey with black-and-white lines. Sexes alike.

Brent goose (*Branta bernicla*): 66cm (26in)
Ranges from the far north of the USA east to Greenland, Iceland and Siberia. Winters further south in Britain and adjacent parts of north-western Europe, as well as in eastern Asia and US coastline. Has a black head and neck, with a trace of white on the side of the neck. Wings are greyish-black. Barred underparts are dark with white markings. Abdomen is white. Sexes are alike.

Canada goose

Branta canadensis

There are a number of different races of Canada goose and these all differ a little in plumage and size. This species has proved to be highly adaptable. Its numbers have grown considerably in Europe, especially in farming areas, where these geese descend in flocks to feed on crops during the winter once other food has become more scarce. When migrating, flocks fly in a clear V-shaped formation. In common with many waterfowl, Canada geese are not able to fly when moulting, but they take readily to the water at this time and can dive if necessary to escape danger. The geese prefer to graze on land, returning to the relative safety of the water during the hours of darkness.

Identification: Distinctive black head and neck. A small area of white plumage runs in a stripe from behind the eyes to under the throat. A whitish area of feathering at the base of the neck merges into brown on the chest. The wings are dark brown and there is white on the abdomen. The legs and feet are blackish. Sexes are alike.

Distribution: Throughout the far north of the Americas, wintering in the southern USA. European population occurs in the British Isles and elsewhere in north-western Europe.
Size: 55–110cm (22–43in).
Habitat: Very variable, but usually near water.
Nest: Vegetation on the ground.
Eggs: 4–7, whitish.
Food: Vegetarian.

Snow goose

Anser caerulescens

Although considered a vagrant rather than a regular visitor to north-western parts of Europe, the snow goose is a relatively common sight in some areas during the winter months. They are especially attracted to farmland, where grazing opportunities are plentiful, and this appears to be helping these birds to extend their range. As with all waterfowl, however, there is always the possibility that sightings of snow geese could represent escapees from waterfowl collections, rather than wild individuals. The calls of snow geese have been likened to the barking of a dog.

Above: Blue snow geese are much less common than their white counterparts.

Identification: Blue-phase birds (above) are dark and blackish, with white heads and white borders to some wing feathers. Young birds of this colour phase have dark heads. White-phase birds (left) are almost entirely white, with dark primary wing feathers. Young of this colour phase have greyish markings on their heads. Sexes alike.

Distribution: Mainly far north of the Americas, Greenland and north-eastern Siberia, but frequently overwinters in Great Britain and nearby coastal areas of north-western Europe.
Size: 84cm (33in).
Habitat: Tundra and coastal lowland agricultural areas.
Nest: Depression lined with vegetation.
Eggs: 4–10, whitish.
Food: Vegetarian.

DUCKS

Waterfowl are generally conspicuous birds on water, but their appearance and distribution can differ markedly through the year. Drakes often resemble hens outside the breeding season, and their plumage is much plainer at this time. Some species are migratory, heading south to escape freezing conditions, although others may be found on stretches of water that could be covered in ice for some periods.

Mallard

Anas platyrhynchos

Distribution: Occurs throughout the Northern Hemisphere and resident through western Europe. Also occurs in North Africa.
Size: 60cm (24in).
Habitat: Open areas of water.
Nest: Scrape lined with down feathers.
Eggs: 7–16, buff to greyish green.
Food: Plant matter and some invertebrates.

These ducks are a common sight, even on stretches of water in towns and cities, such as rivers and canals. They may congregate in quite large flocks, especially outside the breeding season, but they are most evident in the spring, when groups of unpaired males chase potential mates. The nest is often constructed close to water and is frequently hidden under vegetation, especially in urban areas. These birds feed both on water, upending themselves or dabbling at the surface, and on land.

Identification: Metallic-green head with a white ring around the neck. Chest is brownish with grey underparts, and blackish area surrounds the vent. Bluish speculum in the wing, most evident in flight, bordered by black-and-white stripes. Hen is brownish buff overall with darker patterning, and displays same wing markings as drake. Hen's bill is orange, whereas that of male in eclipse plumage (outside the breeding season) is yellow, with a rufous tinge to the breast.

Ruddy shelduck

Tadorna ferruginea

Although these ducks are resident in some parts of their range throughout the year, they are more often migratory. Occasionally, they may be encountered well outside their natural range, and there have been verified sightings reported from countries as far apart as Iceland, Oman and Kenya. They are quite noisy birds by nature, and the calls of drakes are of a higher pitch than those of hens. These shelducks favour stretches of water surrounded by open countryside, allowing them to graze on the surrounding vegetation. Huge flocks may assemble in some areas where conditions are favourable for feeding after the breeding season.

Identification: Cinnamon shade to the head, with paler whitish area around the eyes. Black neck ring; remainder of the body is orange-brown. Greenish gloss to black feathering on the rump. Tail and flight feathers are black. Bill, legs and feet are black. White under the wings. Hens lack the neck collar, which is less apparent in drakes outside the breeding season.

Distribution: North-western Africa, south-western Europe and Asia. Overwinters in eastern Africa.
Size: 70cm (27.5in).
Habitat: Inland, can be some distance from water.
Nest: Down-lined under cover.
Eggs: 8–15, creamy white
Food: Aquatic creatures and plant matter.

Shoveler

Northern shoveler *Anas clypeata*

The broad bill of these waterfowl enables them to feed more easily in shallow water. They typically swim with their bill open, trailing it through the water to catch invertebrates, although they also forage both by upending and catching insects on reeds. Shovelers choose wet ground, often some distance from open water, as a nesting site, where the female retreats from the attention of other drakes. Like the young of other waterfowl, young shovelers take to the water soon after hatching.

Identification: Dark metallic-green head and orange eye. White chest and chestnut-brown flanks and belly, and a black area around the tail. Both back and wings are black and white. The remainder of the body is predominantly white. Broad blue wing stripe, which enables drakes to be recognized even in eclipse plumage, when they resemble hens. Very broad black bill. Hens are predominantly brownish, but with darker blotching. Yellowish edges on the bill and paler area of plumage on the sides of the tail feathers.

Distribution: Widely distributed throughout the Northern Hemisphere, overwintering as far south as central Africa.
Size: 52cm (20in).
Habitat: Shallow coastal and freshwater areas.
Nest: Down-lined scrape.
Eggs: 8–12, green to buff white.
Food: Aquatic invertebrates and plant matter.

Teal (green-winged teal, *Anas crecca*): 38cm (15in)
Found throughout Europe. Resident in the west, migrating south to parts of northern Africa. Also found in Asia and North America. Brown head with broad green stripes running across the eyes and yellow stripes above and below. Chest is pale yellow with black dots. Body and wings are greyish with a yellow area under the tail, and a white edge to the sides of the wings. Hens are mottled brown, with a pale whitish area beneath the tail and a green area on the wing. Bill is dark. Drakes in eclipse plumage resemble hens.

Garganey (*Anas querquedula*): 41cm (16in)
Ranges from England and France eastwards across Europe, overwintering south of the Sahara; present in Asia. Prominent white stripe from the eyes down along the neck. Remainder of the face and breast area are brown with black barring. Greyish area on the body. Wings are greyish black. Brown mottling over the hindquarters. Hens have mottled plumage with a distinctive buff-white area under the chin. Drakes in eclipse plumage resemble hens but with greyish areas on the wings.

Ferruginous duck (*Aythya nyroca*): 42cm (17in)
Occurs throughout much of eastern Europe into Asia, overwintering around the Mediterranean and further south in Africa, as well as in parts of southern Asia. Chestnut plumage, lighter on the flanks than the back, with white eyes. Very obvious white wing stripe. Whitish belly, underwing and undertail area. Greyish bill, black at the tip. Hens are similar but have a pale band across the bill and brown eyes (which distinguishes them from drakes in eclipse plumage).

Pintail (northern pintail, *Anas acuta*): 62cm (24in)
Throughout the Northern Hemisphere, migrating south for the winter to central Africa. Long, narrow black tail. Head is blackish, with white stripes on the neck down to the breast and underparts. Grey flanks. Wings are greyish with prominent wing stripes. Hens are brown, with darker patterning on the plumage and a long, pointed tail with a white edge to the wings in flight.

Pochard

Aythya ferina

These diving ducks are most likely to be seen in areas of open water, where they often dive for food. Stretches of water with islands are favoured, however, as these areas provide relatively secure nesting sites, particularly if there is over-hanging vegetation. Pairs stay together during the nesting period. After that, pochards form larger flocks, sometimes moving away from lakes and similar stretches of still water to nearby rivers, especially when it is likely that ice will form on the water's surface.

Distribution: Resident in parts of western Europe, extending eastwards into Asia and overwintering as far south as Africa.
Size: 49cm (19in).
Habitat: Marshland and lakes.
Nest: Down-lined under cover.
Eggs: 6–14, greenish grey.
Food: Aquatic creatures and plant matter.

Identification: Chestnut-brown head and neck, with black chest and a broad grey band encircling the wings and body. Black feathering surrounds the hindquarters. Eyes are reddish. Black areas are replaced by greyish tone in eclipse plumage. Hens are significantly duller in coloration, with a brownish head with buff areas and notably a stripe extending back from the eyes. Brown also replaces the drake's black plumage.

OWLS

Although owls tend to be nocturnal by nature, the snowy owl, which inhabits the far north where there is almost constant daylight during the summer, hunts during the day. Owls are predatory birds, and it is possible to discover their diet by examining their pellets, which are made up of the indigestible remains of their prey regurgitated after a meal.

Tawny owl

Strix aluco

The distinctive double call notes of these owls reveal their presence, even when it may be hard to spot them because of their dark coloration. They prefer old woodland, where trees tend to be large enough to provide hollow nesting cavities, although tawny owls will adapt to using nest boxes, which has helped to increase their numbers in some areas. Nocturnal by nature, these owls may occasionally hunt during the daytime, especially when they have chicks in the nest. They usually sit quietly on a perch, waiting to swoop down on their quarry. Young tawny owls are unable to fly when they first leave the nest, and adults are very aggressive at this time to protect their offspring.

Identification:
Tawny brown with white markings across the wings, and darker striations over the wings and body. Slight barring on the tail. Distinctive white stripes above the facial disc, which is almost plain brown. Some individuals have a greyer tone to their plumage, while others have a more rufous feathering. The bill is yellowish brown. Sexes are similar, although females are generally larger and heavier. Females can be distinguished by their song, which is a higher pitch.

Distribution: Across Europe (not Ireland) to Scandinavia and east to Asia. Also occurs in western North Africa.
Size: 43cm (17in).
Habitat: Ancient temperate woodland.
Nest: Tree holes.
Eggs: 2–9, white.
Food: Small mammals, birds and invertebrates.

Barn owl

Tyto alba

These owls will roost in dark environments, and have adapted to using buildings for this purpose in various parts of their range. They may be seen in open country, swooping over farmland, with some individuals choosing to pursue bats in areas where the mammals are common. Males in particular will often utter harsh screeches when in flight, which serve as territorial markers, while females make a distinctive snoring sound for food at the nest site. They pair for life, which can be more than 20 years. Barn owls have adapted to hunting alongside roadside verges, but here they risk being hit by vehicles.

Distribution: Worldwide. Throughout western Europe, Africa (apart from the Sahara) and the Middle East.
Size: 39cm (15in).
Habitat: Prefers relatively open countryside.
Nest: Hollow tree or inside a building.
Eggs: 4–7, white.
Food: Voles, amphibians and invertebrates.

Identification: Very pale in colour, with whitish, heart-shaped face and underparts, although in northern, central and eastern parts of Europe, the underparts have a decidedly yellowish-orange tone. Top of the head and wings are greyish with spots evident. Eyes are black. Male birds are often paler than females.

Little owl (*Athene noctua*): 27cm (11in)
Ranges across western Europe and Asia, and from northern Africa to the Middle East. Was successfully introduced to the British Isles in the late 1800s, and now occurs in England and Wales. Has a large, round, brown head with white eyebrows. Head and wings are spotted with white. Pale underparts are streaked with brown. Has a pale bill. The iris is yellow. Hens may be slightly bigger.

Great grey owl (*Strix nebulosa*): 68cm (27in)
Circumpolar, from Scandinavia east through Asia, and also across most of North America. Greyish overall with darker streaking on the wings and underparts. Fine circular patterning of grey lines on the face, with highly distinctive white half-circles extending around the inner side of the eyes, which are yellow. White line of patterning also apparent on the wings. Hens may be slightly bigger.

Long-eared owl (*Asio otus*): 37cm (14.5in)
Ranges from mainland Europe across Asia. Also found in western North Africa and North America. Characteristic tufts on the head are only raised when the owl is alert. The facial area is an orangish-yellow with a white central area extending between the orange eyes and around the bill. Underparts are pale yellow with black streaking. Hens have more rusty-buff faces, otherwise sexes are alike.

Eagle owl

Eurasian eagle owl *Bubo bubo*

The scientific name of the eagle owl – *Bubo bubo* – reflects the sound of its calls, which can be audible on still nights from quite a distance away. A pair will call alternately before mating, and the call notes of the female are higher in pitch. In spite of their large size, these owls fly quietly and may sometimes be seen soaring. Formidable hunters, they take large, potentially dangerous quarry, attacking buzzards and herons on occasion. Even so, eagle owls have adaptable feeding habits, and may resort to catching earthworms and fish as well as eating carrion when hunting opportunities are limited.

Distribution: Throughout southern Europe, north to Scandinavia and east across Asia. Small populations in parts of western Europe and western North Africa.
Size: 73cm (29in).
Habitat: Rocky areas, relatively open country.
Nest: Cliff ledges or occasionally on the ground.
Eggs: 1–4, white.
Food: Mammals and birds.

Identification: Brownish with dark markings on the wings. Underparts are buff brown with streaking most evident on the breast. Prominent ear tufts. Black bill. Orange iris. Hens are often slightly bigger. There may be great variation in appearance through their wide range, with at least 13 different varieties being recognized.

Snowy owl

Nyctea scandiaca

The plumage of these owls enables them to blend in well in the tundra region where they commonly occur. In this harsh environment, their numbers are closely related to the availability of their prey, and their population increases rapidly when lemmings are rife. Once the lemming population declines, however, so does that of the snowy owls, and breeding success is greatly reduced, so that pairs may not nest at all in some years. Adult birds are likely to be forced to abandon their usual territories at this time and have to fly south in search of other sources of food. Unusually, snowy owls are active during the daytime.

Distribution: Circumpolar in the Northern Hemisphere, moving further south in winter.
Size: 65cm (25.5in).
Habitat: Woodland, extending to the tundra.
Nest: Scrape on the ground.
Eggs: 3–11, white.
Food: Mainly lemmings but also birds, invertebrates and fish.

Identification: Cocks are white with yellow eyes and feathering down to the claws. Hens have brown barring all over their bodies apart from their faces, which are white. Young are similar to hens.

CUCKOOS AND WOODPECKERS

These groups of birds have adapted in different ways to survive in colder northern climates, where invertebrates are in short supply during the winter months. While members of the cuckoo clan migrate south to Africa for the winter, where they can find sufficient invertebrates, woodpeckers rely mainly on seeds and nuts for food during this period.

Cuckoo

Common cuckoo *Cuculus canorus*

The distinctive call of the common cuckoo has traditionally been regarded as one of the earliest signs of spring in Europe, when these birds return from their African wintering grounds. Typically, these cuckoos are resident in Europe only between April and September. Adult cuckoos have an unusual ability to feed on hairy caterpillars, which are often plentiful in woodland areas through much of the summer. Common cuckoos are parasitic in their breeding habits, with hens laying single eggs in the nests of other smaller birds such as hedge sparrows, wagtails and meadow pipits. The unsuspecting hosts hatch a monster in their midst, with the cuckoo chick throwing eggs or potential rivals out of the nest in order to monopolize the food supply.

Right: The young cuckoo lifts eggs on its back to eject them from the nest.

Identification: Grey head, upper chest, wings and tail, and black edging to the white feathers of the underparts. In hens this barring extends virtually up to the throat, offset against a more yellowish background. Some hens belong to a brown colour morph, with rufous feathering replacing grey, and black barring apparent on the upperparts.

Distribution: Across Europe and east to Asia. Also present in North Africa. Northern European birds overwinter in eastern and southern parts of Africa, while Asiatic birds range out to the Philippines.
Size: 36cm (14in).
Habitat: Wide range, thanks to host species.
Nest: Parasitizes that of host species.
Eggs: 1 per nest, resembles that of its host.
Food: Invertebrates, including caterpillars.

Nightjar

European nightjar *Caprimulgus europaeus*

The nightjar is a regular summertime visitor to Europe. Their nocturnal habits make these birds difficult to observe, but they have very distinctive calls that have been likened both to the croaking of a frog and the noise of a machine. The calls are uttered for long periods and carry over a distance of 1km (0.6m). Even during the daytime, the mottled plumage of these birds provides them with excellent camouflage, especially in woodland, particularly as they usually narrow their eyes to slits, which further conceals their presence. Nightjars spend much of their time resting on the ground during the daytime, but are sufficiently agile to catch moths and beetles in flight after dark. These birds may sometimes be seen hunting night-flying invertebrates. If food is plentiful, a pair may nest twice in succession before migrating south.

Identification: Fine bill. Long wings. Greyish-brown mottled appearance overall, with some black areas too, especially near the shoulder. White areas below the eyes and on the wings, although white spots on the wings are seen only in cock birds.

Distribution: Europe and North Africa, east to Asia. Northern European birds overwinter in central and southern parts of Africa, and those found in the south migrate to western Africa.
Size: 28cm (11in).
Habitat: Heathland and relatively open country.
Nest: Scrape on the ground.
Eggs: 2, buff with darker markings.
Food: Invertebrates.

Great spotted cuckoo

Clamator glandarius

These lively cuckoos will hunt for invertebrates in trees and on the ground, hopping along rather clumsily. Great spotted cuckoos are bold by nature, parasitizing the nests of magpies and similar corvids, as well as sometimes laying in the nests of starlings in Africa. The hen usually removes eggs already present in the host bird's nest before laying, but if any remain and hatch, the nestlings are reared alongside the young cuckoos. Their relatively large size and noisy nature make these cuckoos quite conspicuous, particularly after the breeding period, when they form flocks.

Identification: Silvery grey top to the head with slight crest. Darker grey neck, back and wings, with white spots over the wings. Pale yellow plumage under the throat extending to the upper breast. The remainder of the underparts are white. Sexes alike, although their song notes are different. Young birds are much darker in colour – black rather than grey with rusty brown flight feathers.

Distribution: Ranges throughout southern Europe from Spain to Iran in Asia. Migrates to north-eastern and southern Africa.
Size: 39cm (15in).
Habitat: Relatively open country.
Nest: Parasitizes that of host species.
Eggs: 1 per nest, resembles those of the host.
Food: Invertebrates.

Senegal coucal (*Centropus senegalensis*): 40cm (16in)
Ranges across Africa from Senegal to Sudan and Tanzania. Also present in Egypt and southern Africa. Strong bill, with black plumage extending over the head down the neck. Underparts are lemon. Back is dark brown. Wings are rusty brown and tail is long and black. Sexes alike.

Lesser spotted woodpecker (*Dendrocopos minor*): 16cm (6in)
Ranges across most of Europe, south to Algeria and Tunisia, east into Asia. Buff area above the bill. Males have a red area on the crown; hens have black. Black tail, white barring on wings. Barring on underparts with reddish area around the vent. Black stripes on the sides of the face.

Green woodpecker (European green woodpecker, *Picus viridis*): 36cm (14in)
Found throughout Europe (except Scotland and Ireland), east to Asia. Red plumage from above the bill down the nape. Black area around the eyes. Greyish area on the throat. Underparts are greyish green. Upperparts are more greenish with yellower tone on the rump. Cocks have red centres to the black streak below the lower bill.

Wryneck (Eurasian wryneck, *Jynx torquilla*): 18cm (7in)
Present across much of Europe and North Africa, migrating south for the winter. Has mottled grey plumage on the head and over the back and a barred tail. There is a brownish tone on the wings and a dark stripe running across and behind the eyes. Throat and upper breast are buff streaked with black. The underparts are whitish with dark barring. Sexes are alike.

Great spotted woodpecker

Picoides major

Identification: A black area runs from the bill around the sides of the neck and links with a red area at the back. Wings and upper tail are predominantly black, although there is a white area on the wings and barring on the flight feathers. There is a deep red area around the vent and large white spots on the underside of the tail. Hens lack the red area on the hindcrown.

These woodpeckers are likely to be seen in both coniferous and deciduous woodland habitats, especially in areas where the trees are mature enough for the birds to excavate chambers for roosting and nesting. Their powerful bill enables them to extract grubs concealed under bark and to wrest the seeds from pine cones – the birds use so-called "anvils", which may be existing tree holes, as vices to hold the cones fast so as to gain more leverage for their bills.

Distribution: Most of Europe (except Ireland and the far north of Scandinavia). Also found in North Africa. Ranges east into Asia.
Size: 25cm (10in).
Habitat: Woodland.
Nest: Tree hollows.
Eggs: 5–7, white.
Food: Invertebrates, eggs and seeds.

CORVIDS

Studies suggest that corvids rank among the most intelligent avian species. Many of these birds display an instinctive desire to hoard food, such as acorns, to help sustain them through the winter months. Their plumage is often predominantly black, sometimes with grey and white areas. Corvids are generally noisy and quite aggressive by nature.

Magpie

Common magpie *Pica pica*

Bold and garrulous, magpies are a common sight throughout much of their range. They are often blamed for the decline of songbirds because of their habit of raiding the nests of other birds. They are usually seen in small groups, although pairs will nest on their own. If a predator such as a cat ventures close to the nest, there will be a considerable commotion, resulting in the nesting magpies being joined by others in the neighbourhood to harry the unfortunate feline. Magpies sometimes take an equally direct approach when seeking food, chasing other birds, gulls in particular, to make them drop their food. Magpies are quite agile when walking, holding their long tails up as they move.

Identification: Black head, upper breast, back, rump and tail, with a broad white patch around the abdomen. Broad white wing stripe and dark blue areas evident below on folded wings. Depending on the light, there may be a green gloss apparent on the black plumage. Sexes alike, but the cock may have a longer tail.

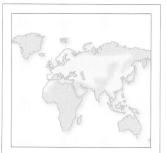

Distribution: Much of Europe and south to North Africa. Represented in parts of Asia and North America.
Size: 51cm (20in).
Habitat: Trees with surrounding open areas.
Nest: Dome-shaped stick pile.
Eggs: 2–8, bluish green with darker markings.
Food: Omnivorous.

Nutcracker (spotted nutcracker, *Nucifraga caryocatactes*): 35cm (14in)
Present in Scandinavia and southwards and eastwards into Asia. Dark brown crown, with white-speckled brown plumage over the body, apart from a white area around the vent and the brownish-black wings. Sexes are alike.

Jackdaw (western jackdaw, *Corvus monedula*): 34cm (13in)
Ranges throughout western Europe and North Africa. Present in southern Scandinavia and east into Asia. Dark grey, lighter on the neck. Eye is pale blue. Relatively short bill. Sexes are alike.

Carrion crow (*Corvus corone*): 51cm (20in)
Found in western and south-western parts of Europe. Has black plumage that sometimes appears slightly glossy. The broad, blunt bill is curved on its upper surface, with no bare skin at the base and feathering around the nostrils. Sexes are alike.

Red-billed chough (*Pyrrhocorax pyrrhocorax*): 80cm (31in)
Small populations are found on cliffs of south-western and western parts of Britain. Also found in Ireland and around the Mediterranean. Glossy black plumage with a distinctive, curved, narrow red bill. Legs and feet are pinkish. Sexes are alike.

Jay

Eurasian jay *Garrulus glandarius*

Throughout their wide range, there is some local variation in the appearance of these jays, both in the depth of colour and the amount of black on the top of the head. However, their harsh call, which resembles a hoarse scream, coupled with a flash of colour, help identify them. Jays are shy by nature and rarely allow a close approach. They store acorns and other seeds in the autumn, and such caches help to sustain them through the winter when the ground may be covered in snow, restricting their opportunities to find other food. During the summer, these jays may raid the nests of other birds, taking both eggs and chicks.

Distribution: Throughout most of Europe (except Scotland and the extreme north of Scandinavia). Also present in North Africa and Asia.
Size: 35cm (14in).
Habitat: Woodland.
Nest: Platform of twigs.
Eggs: 3–7, bluish green with dense speckling.
Food: Omnivorous.

Identification: Pinkish brown with a greyer shade on the wings. Streaking on the head. Broad, black moustachial stripe with whitish throat. White rump and undertail area. Tail is dark. White stripe on the wings with black and blue markings on the sides of the wings. Sexes alike.

Rook

Corvus frugilegus

These highly social corvids nest in colonies, partly because they inhabit areas of open countryside where there are few trees available. There is, nevertheless, a strong bond between the members of a pair. The rookery serves as the group's centre, which makes them vulnerable to human persecution, but although they eat corn, they are valued for consuming invertebrates as well. The rook's bill is adapted to digging in the ground to extract invertebrates, especially cranefly ("daddy-long-legs") larvae. Outside the breeding season, it is not uncommon for rooks to associate with other corvids, such as jackdaws, crows and ravens, as an alternative to the rookery may be used as a roosting site at this time.

Distribution: Throughout Europe east to Asia. Some populations move south in the winter to the north Mediterranean.
Size: 49cm (19in).
Habitat: Close to farmland.
Nest: Made of sticks built in trees.
Eggs: 2–7, bluish green with dark markings.
Food: Omnivorous, but mainly invertebrates.

Identification: Entirely black plumage, with a pointed bill that has bare, pinkish skin at its base. The nostrils of adult rooks are unfeathered, distinguishing them from carrion crows. Rooks also have a flatter forehead and a peak to the crown. Sexes alike.

Raven

Common raven *Corvus corax*

Distribution: Mainly south-western Europe and North Africa north to Scandinavia and east throughout most of northern Asia. Also present in North America, Greenland, Iceland and the British Isles.
Size: 67cm (26in).
Habitat: Relatively open country.
Nest: Bulky, made of sticks.
Eggs: 3–7, bluish with darker spots.
Food: Carrion.

Identification: Very large in size with a powerful, curved bill. Entirely black plumage. Wedge-shaped tail in flight, when the flight feathers stand out, creating a fingered appearance at the tips. Males often larger than females.

The croaking calls of the raven are a foolproof way of identifying this bird, and its size is also a good identifier. Ravens are the largest members of the crow family occurring in the Northern Hemisphere. The impression of bulk conveyed by these birds is reinforced by their shaggy throat feathers, which do not lie sleekly. There is a recognized decline in size across their range, with ravens found in the far north larger than those occurring further south. Pairs occupy relatively large territories, and even outside the breeding season they tend not to associate in large flocks. When searching for food, ravens are able to fly quite effortlessly over long distances, flapping their wings slowly.

VULTURES AND EAGLES

As a result of their size, these large birds of prey are usually quite conspicuous in flight. Population densities are quite low, however, and these birds have often suffered great persecution by people because of fears that the birds will attack domestic stocks of fish and farm animals. They tend to be quite scarce, therefore, and today are observed mainly in more remote areas of countryside.

Griffon vulture

Eurasian vulture *Gyps fulvus*

These vultures are most likely to be seen in areas of relatively open countryside with surrounding cliffs and these are used for nesting and roosting. They glide over plains, using their keen eyesight to help them locate carcasses, although, these days groups of these birds may often be encountered scavenging at rubbish dumps within their range. Hot currents of air, known as thermals, enable these vultures to soar and remain airborne with little effort. Griffon vultures nest in colonies that have been known to consist of as many as 150 pairs. Chicks develop slowly, often not embarking on their first flight until they are nearly 20 weeks old. Young birds are unlikely to breed until they are at least four years old.

Identification: Dark brown area on the head around the eyes, with the top of the head and neck whitish. Light brown body, back and wings, darker flight feathers and tail. Relatively elongated horn-coloured bill that is curved on the upper tip. Legs and feet grey, and whitish on the inner thighs. Sexes are alike. Young birds have a darker brown back and a brown neck collar. Can be distinguished from the African white-backed vulture (*G. africanis*) by its larger size and paler plumage.

Distribution: The Iberian Peninsula and western North Africa, east into Asia and the Middle East. Young birds may migrate further south into western and eastern Africa.
Size: 110cm (43in).
Habitat: Mountain country.
Nest: Sticks on rocky crag.
Eggs: 1, white with reddish-brown markings.
Food: Carrion.

Osprey

Pandion haliaetus

The distribution of the osprey extends naturally to all inhabited continents, making it one of the most widely distributed of all birds. They have adapted to feeding on stretches of fresh water as well as on estuaries and even the open sea, swooping to grab fish from just below the water's surface using their powerful talons. Ospreys are capable of carrying fish typically weighing up to 300g (11oz) without difficulty. In many areas, especially in Europe, ospreys are migratory, and the birds head south to Africa for the duration of the northern winter. Those occurring in Scotland and Scandinavia fly south of the Sahara, rather than joining the resident osprey population in North Africa.

Left: Osprey feed only on fish, pouncing on those just below the surface.

Identification: Brown stripes running across the eyes down over the back and wings. Eyes are yellow. Top of the head and underparts are white, with brown striations across the breast, which are most marked in hens. Tall, upright stance, powerful grey legs and talons. Hens significantly heavier than cocks.

Distribution: Global, with European ospreys ranging from parts of Scandinavia west to the British Isles and south to the Iberian Peninsula and other areas in Europe. Widely distributed in the winter in Africa south of the Sahara.
Size: 58cm (23in).
Habitat: Close to stretches of water.
Nest: Platform of sticks in a tree.
Eggs: 3, white with darker markings.
Food: Fish.

Black vulture (Eurasian black vulture, *Aegypius monachus*): 107cm (42in)
Ranges from Spain and the Balearic Islands eastwards to the Balkans, and from Turkey across Asia. Some birds overwinter in north-eastern Africa. Pale bluish skin encircles the nostrils. Bald head with a brownish area around the eyes. Plumage is a dark sooty black. Sexes are alike.

Egyptian vulture (*Neophron percnopterus*): 70cm (27.5in)
Distributed around the Mediterranean into Asia, on to the Canary Islands and south of the Sahara and across Africa to Tanzania and Arabia. Pale-coloured, whitish plumage with brown markings is prominent over the wings and flight feathers. Has a bald bright yellow area of skin on the sides of the face and along the bill, which may have a dark tip. Sexes are alike.

Short-toed snake eagle (*Circaetus gallicus*): 67cm (26in)
Ranges across mainland Europe north to Finland and east to Asia. Also present in western North Africa. Birds from western Europe migrate south to the Sahel region in West Africa. Has a mottled brown head and wings and this extends to the breast. The underparts are white with brown barring. The flight feathers are a darker brown and the tail is barred. Sexes are alike.

Lesser spotted eagle (*Aquila pomarina*): 64cm (25in)
Ranges from eastern Europe to Turkey and around the Caspian Sea. Overwinters in eastern Africa. Chocolate brown. Feathering extends to the feet. Bill is yellow at base with a dark tip. Sexes alike.

Golden eagle

Aquila chrysaetos

These eagles generally inhabit remote areas away from people, where they are likely to be left undisturbed. When seen in flight, the golden eagle's head looks relatively small compared to its broad tail and large, square-ended wings. Although it has some yapping call notes not unlike those of a dog, its calls are generally quite shrill. Its hunting skills are well adapted to its environment. In some areas, for instance, the golden eagle takes tortoises, dropping the reptiles from a great height in order to smash their shells before eating them; in other areas, they may prey on cats. They prefer to capture their quarry on the ground, swooping down low, rather than catching birds in the air.

Identification: Brown overall, with yellowish-brown plumage restricted to the back of the head, extending down the nape of the neck. Eagles inhabiting desert areas, such as the Middle East, tend to be slightly paler overall. Bill is yellow with a dark tip. Feet are yellow with black talons. Hens are bigger than cocks.

Distribution: Sporadic through the Mediterranean area into Asia. Present in Scotland, Scandinavia and eastwards into Asia. Also occurs in North Africa.
Size: 90cm (35in).
Habitat: Mountainous areas.
Nest: Massive cliff nest made of sticks.
Eggs: 2, white with dark markings.
Food: Mainly birds and mammals.

Imperial eagle

Eastern imperial eagle *Aquila heliaca* (E)

The population of these eagles declined dramatically during the 20th century because of persecution by humans. Thanks to effective protection, however, there are now signs that their numbers are increasing again in areas such as Hungary. Here they can be seen in areas of open countryside, rather than retreating to the relative safety of mountain forests, away from persecution. Imperial eagles, like others of their kind, are potentially long-lived birds, having few natural enemies apart from people. Their longevity, which is measured in decades not years, is mirrored in their development. Young birds may not breed for the first time until they are six years old, when they are still likely to be in immature plumage.

Identification: Mainly dark brown, with a paler buff area at the back of the head extending down around the neck. Restricted patches of white appear in the shoulder area. The bill is yellow with a dark tip and the feet are yellow. Sexes alike. This species is now regarded as distinct from the Spanish imperial eagle (*A. adalberti*), which has small white shoulder patches.

Distribution: Eastern Europe into Turkey and east across much of Central Asia. Migrates south to eastern Africa and Arabia as well as to parts of Asia for the winter.
Size: 84cm (33in).
Habitat: Prefers open country.
Nest: Made of sticks and other vegetation.
Eggs: 2, white with dark markings.
Food: Small mammals, birds and carrion.

HAWKS AND HARRIERS

These predatory birds can be easily identified by their sharp, pointed bills and powerful talons. They prey on both other birds and mammals, with some resorting to carrion and invertebrates. There are recognized colour variants, known as morphs, which may cause the plumage of some individuals to be either lighter or darker than usual.

Red kite

Milvus milvus

Distribution: Wales, Iberian Peninsula and the adjacent area of North Africa. Extends north-east across Europe to southern Sweden and into the Caucasus.
Size: 66cm (26in).
Habitat: Lightly wooded areas.
Nest: Platform made of sticks in a tree.
Eggs: 1–4, white with reddish-brown markings.
Food: Small birds, mammals and carrion.

Although they are very agile hunters, red kites also seek out carrion such as dead sheep. This behaviour has resulted in their persecution in some areas because of misplaced fears that these birds actually kill lambs. When seeking prey, red kites will circle repeatedly over an area, relying on their keen eyesight to spot movement on the ground. They then drop and sweep low to home in on their target. Up until the 1700s, flocks of red kites were common scavengers on the streets of London where they were sufficiently tame to swoop down and steal food from children. It was their propensity to scavenge, however, that led to a dramatic reduction in their numbers as they were easily killed using carcasses laced with poison.

Identification: Predominantly reddish brown, with a greyish head streaked with darker markings. Darker mottling over the wings, with some variable streaking on the underparts as well. Feet are yellowish with black talons. White area under the wings and forked tail can be clearly seen in flight. Sexes alike.

Hen harrier

Northern harrier *Circus cyaneus*

Hen harriers have a very distinctive hunting pattern. They fly low over moorland, seeking not just small mammals but also birds such as grouse, which has led to their persecution by gamekeepers in various parts of their range. Over the winter period, however, these harriers may be forced to feed largely on carrion. Their range extends further north than that of related species, into tundra regions. However, they are not resident in far northern regions throughout the year, and head south before the start of winter in the Northern Hemisphere. Hen harriers are unusual in that they not only frequently roost but also breed on the ground. After the breeding season, they often congregate at communal sites, which are used for several generations.

Identification: Mainly chestnut streaked with white. Darker over the wings. Narrow white band around the eye, with a solid brown area beneath. Has a barred tail, a dark bill and yellow legs. Hens are larger.

Distribution: Throughout much of the Northern Hemisphere. Extends across most of Europe, including Scandinavia, east to Asia. Often moves south for the winter as far as North Africa.
Size: 52cm (20in).
Habitat: Moorland.
Nest: On the ground, hidden in vegetation.
Eggs: 3–5, whitish.
Food: Small mammals and birds.

Common buzzard

Eurasian buzzard *Buteo buteo*

With its rather stocky and broad appearance, the buzzard's silhouette in flight helps to confirm its identity. Buzzards are capable of soaring for long periods before suddenly swooping down to seize creatures such as rabbits, which are its traditional prey, particularly in many parts of Europe. At the other extreme, buzzards can also sometimes be observed hunting invertebrates, walking purposefully on the ground in search of their quarry. They may even be spotted on roads on occasion, feeding on road kill, and sometimes even placing themselves in danger from passing traffic. Buzzards remain one of the most common raptors in Europe, however, thanks in part to their adaptability.

Identification: Mainly dark brown, with a variable amount of white plumage around the bill and on the underparts. The tail is barred with paler plumage around the vent. The legs and feet are yellow and the bill is yellow with a dark tip. White plumage predominates in the pale morph. Hens are often larger.

Distribution: Resident in western Europe. Summer resident in parts of Scandinavia and east across Asia. European migratory birds overwinter in parts of southern and eastern Africa.
Size: 57cm (22in).
Habitat: Areas with trees.
Nest: Platform made of sticks, usually in a tree.
Eggs: 2–4, white.
Food: Small mammals and other prey.

Black kite (*Milvus migrans*): 60cm (24in)
Present on much of mainland Europe to Asia and Australia. Also occurs in North Africa and over-winters in Africa south of the Sahara. Mainly brown but darker on the wings. The underparts are decidedly rufous. Barring on the tail. Some grey markings on the head. Sexes are alike.

Common black-shouldered kite (*Elanus caeruleus*): 30cm (12in)
Present in North Africa and widely distributed in Africa south of the Sahara. Grey on the head, extending down the back over the wings. Whitish sides to the face and white underparts. Prominent black area on each wing extending down from the shoulders. Sexes are alike.

Montagu's harrier (*Circus pygargus*): 50cm (20in)
Found in Europe and North Africa and then east to Asia. Overwinters in Central and eastern Africa south of the Sahara. Predominantly grey, with barring on the lower underparts. Has a narrow white rump. Hens are larger and brown areas replace the grey areas of plumage. In the dark morph, males are blackish and hens are a dark chocolate brown.

Goshawk (northern goshawk, *Accipiter gentilis*): 50–68cm (20–27in)
Widely distributed throughout the Northern Hemisphere. Extends across most of Europe into Asia, with a small population in north-western Africa. Also present in North America. Grey on the head, more silvery over the wings and tail. Rest of plumage is mainly white with grey barring. Hens are bigger than cocks. In the rare white morph, birds are much paler than normal.

Sparrowhawk

Eurasian sparrowhawk *Accipiter nisus*

These birds of prey tend to favour birds that feed on the ground, and males tend to take smaller quarry than females, reflecting the difference in their respective sizes. Even females rarely take birds much bigger than pigeons, however, although they will prey on thrushes. Pairs nest later in the year than many songbirds, so that they can prey on nestlings more easily to feed their own chicks. Their short wings mean that sparrowhawks are very agile in flight, able to manoeuvre easily in wooded areas. They approach quietly with the aim of catching their target unawares, and seize their prey using their powerful feet.

Identification: Grey head, back and wings with darker barring on the grey tail. The underparts are barred. Has bare yellow legs and feet with relatively long toes. Cock birds are smaller than hens and have pale rufous areas on the lower sides of the face that extend to the chest. In addition, the barring on their underparts is browner.

Left: Young male sparrow-hawks fledge several days before the heavier females.

Distribution: Resident throughout most of Europe, (apart from the far north of Scandinavia), North Africa and the Canary Islands. Migratory birds overwinter around the Red Sea. Distribution also extends east to Asia.
Size: 28cm (11in).
Habitat: Lightly wooded areas.
Nest: Made of sticks in a tree.
Eggs: 4–6, pale blue with reddish-brown markings.
Food: Mainly birds.

FALCONS

Agile, aerial predators, these birds of prey are opportunistic, relying on their strength and speed to overcome their prey, which frequently includes smaller birds. In the past, falcon populations have been adversely affected by organochlorine pesticides such as DDT, but today there has been a resurgence in numbers in many areas, with populations even moving into urban areas.

Kestrel

Common kestrel *Falco tinnunculus*

These birds of prey are often seen hovering over the sides of busy roads, which provide them with good hunting opportunities. They catch prey largely undisturbed on the roadside as traffic passes by. The keen eyesight of kestrels enables them to spot even small quarry such as grasshoppers on the ground, and in the winter, they may resort to hunting earthworms drawn to the surface by heavy rainfall. Kestrels will also venture into towns, hunting in parks.

Identification: Bluish-grey head, with a black stripe under the eyes and a whitish throat. Has dense black spotting on the pale brownish chest, extending to the abdomen. Wings are chestnut brown with black markings. Rump and tail feathers are grey with black tips. Hens are similar to cocks, but have browner heads and distinct barring across the tail feathers.

Distribution: Throughout western Europe to southern Asia and North Africa. Also breeds in Scandinavia.
Size: 37cm (14.5in).
Habitat: Open countryside.
Nest: Platform made of sticks in a tree or in farm buildings.
Eggs: 3–7, pale pink with dark brown markings.
Food: Invertebrates and small mammals.

Peregrine falcon

Falco peregrinus

The power of the peregrine falcon is such that it can swoop down on other birds at great speed. Indeed, it is thought that they can dive as quickly as 350km/h (217mph). Pigeons are a favourite prey although these falcons may also hunt waterfowl. The impact made by their feet when they strike in the air is so great that their quarry is frequently killed instantaneously. These falcons are highly adaptable and can very occasionally be sighted in cities, where apartment blocks replace the crags from which they would normally fly on hunting excursions.

Identification: Has dark grey upperparts. A broad blackish stripe extends down below the eyes and the surrounding white area extends right around the throat. The barring on the chest is lighter than on the abdomen. Darker markings are apparent on the grey feathers of the back and wings. The tail is barred with paler grey feathering at the base. The legs and feet are yellow. Has relatively narrow wings when seen in flight. Hens are much larger than male birds.

Distribution: Resident throughout most of western Europe and much of Africa, apart from the Sahara Desert and the central rainforest band. One of the most adaptable and widely distributed birds of prey, occurring on all continents.
Size: 38–51cm (15–20in).
Habitat: Usually near cliffs, sometimes open ground.
Nest: Usually on cliff ledges.
Eggs: 3–4, whitish with red-brown markings.
Food: Birds.

Red-footed falcon (*Falco vespertinus*): 34cm (13in)
Mainly found in eastern Europe and Asia but with a few recorded sightings in western Europe, including the British Isles. Predominantly bluish-grey overall with red on the lower abdomen and undertail coverts. The legs are a bright red. Hens are rufous-brown with a white area on the face below the eyes. Their wings are blue-grey with black barring and their legs are pinkish.

Hobby (Eurasian hobby, *Falco subbuteo*): 35cm (14in)
Ranges across most of mainland Europe, north to southern Scandinavia, east to Asia and south to North Africa. Over-winters in southern Africa. Long, pointed, dark bluish-grey wings. A white band extends around the sides of the face. White underparts with barring. Reddish area on the lower abdomen. Barred underside to the tail. Sexes are alike.

Lanner falcon (*Falco biarmicus*): 50cm (20in)
Extends throughout south-eastern Europe, Arabia and much of Africa apart from the central rainforest area. Slaty-grey or brownish-grey upperparts although those from North Africa are a more bluish shade. A dark stripe extends down below the eyes into a whitish area that extends across the cheeks on to the throat. Underparts are white with dark barring. Legs and feet are yellow. Sexes alike but hens are larger.

Saker falcon (*Falco cherrug*): 55cm (22in)
Occurs in central Europe, via Russia eastwards across southern latitudes in Asia, extending to China. Westerly populations may migrate around the eastern Mediterranean and North Africa for the winter. Also observed at this stage in Arabia and eastern Africa, Sudan, Ethiopia and northern parts of Kenya. Predominantly brown with a paler head. Underparts heavily streaked on the breast and darker areas on the flanks. Dark underwing coverts broken with some whitish markings. Sexes are alike. A rare grey morph is also seen occasionally.

Merlin

Pigeon hawk *Falco columbarius*

These highly adaptable hawks can be observed in a wide range of environments. They tend to breed in the far north where there is little cover, swooping low and fast above the ground in search of prey. Pairs may sometimes seek out and pursue their quarry together, increasing their chances of making a kill. Indeed, merlins have even been seen hunting in the company of other birds of prey. The merlin prefers to tackle birds in flight rather than seizing individual birds when they are perching.

Distribution: Present in the British Isles throughout the year. Occurs in Scandinavia, moving south in the winter down to North Africa. Occurs in Asia and the Americas also.
Size: 33cm (13in).
Habitat: Lightly wooded and open countryside.
Nest: In trees or sometimes on the ground.
Eggs: 3–6, buff with variable reddish speckling.
Food: Mostly birds.

Identification: Orange-brown underparts and collar with dark streaking. Crown and wings are bluish-grey with dark streaking. Streaking also on the whitish cheeks. A broad dark band on the tail with a white tip. Hens have brownish-grey upperparts with a series of four or five narrow light bands extending down the tail. Upperparts are whitish with brown markings. Males usually smaller than females.

Gyr falcon

Falco rusticolus

The largest member of its genus, the gyr falcon is well adapted to surviving in the far north, where its coloration helps to conceal its presence, even in areas where there is little tree cover. These falcons are often sighted in coastal regions, where they prey on seabirds. They tend to fly quite low when hunting in open countryside, taking grouse and similar birds as well as small rodents, and prefer to catch their quarry on the ground rather than in flight. When breeding, pairs may even adopt artificial sites, nesting in buildings associated with oil pipelines, for example.

Identification: Variable in colour, but typically bluish-grey with barring across the back and wings. Tail is barred. Sides of the face are dark. Underparts are whitish with dark barring. The white morph (*left*), has white underparts and occurs predominantly in Greenland. Two grey morphs exist: the lighter grey occurs in Iceland and the dark grey in parts of Scandinavia and northern Russia.

Distribution: Iceland and Scandinavia. Annual vagrant in the British Isles.
Size: 63cm (25in)
Habitat: Mainly taiga and tundra.
Nest: On cliff ledges.
Eggs: 3–4, buff with dense reddish speckling.
Food: Small birds and mammals.

AFRICAN PARROTS

Africa is home to just 22 species of parrot – fewer than are found on any other continent where these birds naturally occur. The African population includes island residents such as the echo parakeet (Psittacula echo) from Mauritius, one of the rarest species in the world and a close relative of the ring-necked parakeet, as well as the bizarre, black-coloured vasa parrots found on Madagascar.

Grey parrot

Psittacus erithacus

The highly distinctive coloration of these parrots enables them to be identified without difficulty, although they are not always easy to spot in their forest habitat. They are more conspicuous in the early morning and evening, when they fly above the trees in flocks, often calling loudly, to and from their feeding grounds. These parrots roost in mature trees, giving them a good view of the surrounding area. They are not easy to approach and often fly off at the first hint of danger. When feeding, at least one bird acts as a sentinel, calling loudly to warn the others of any approaching threat.

Identification: Mainly grey (a silvery shade in some cases) with bright red tail feathers. The timneh subspecies (*P. e. timneh*) from western Africa is not only smaller, but has a maroon tail and a horn-coloured, rather than black, upper bill. Sexes are alike.

Distribution: Across central Africa from the Gulf of Guinea east to Kenya and Tanzania. Occurs south to Angola.
Size: 33cm (13in)
Habitat: Woodland areas from rainforest to mangroves and savanna.
Nest: Tree hollow, often 10m (33ft) high or more.
Eggs: 2–3, white.
Food: Fruits, nuts and seeds, often sought in trees.

Senegal parrot

Yellow-bellied parrot *Poicephalus senegalus*

These parrots tend to be observed only in small groups, although much bigger flocks may congregate in areas where food is plentiful, raiding agricultural areas when crops are ripening. Groundnuts are a particular favourite of these parrots. In some areas, such as southern Mali, seasonal movements have been reported, with the parrots heading further south during the dry season, when areas of standing water become scarce. These birds are very shy by nature – they are difficult to observe when they are perched and fly off rapidly when disturbed. At such times their calls, which frequently consist of whistling notes, become more raucous.

Identification: Has a greyish head with a green back and wings. Has a distinctive V-shaped green area on the chest, with orangish-yellow plumage beneath. The distinctive western subspecies (*P. s. versteri*) has more reddish underparts and darker green plumage. Sexes are alike.

Distribution: Western central parts of Africa, extending from Senegal to northern parts of Cameroon and south-east of Chad.
Size: 23cm (9in).
Habitat: Open countryside and forest.
Nest: Tree hollow, typically 10m (33ft) off the ground.
Eggs: 2–4, white.
Food: Fruit, greenstuff, seeds and cultivated crops, especially groundnuts and millet.

Peach-faced lovebird

Rosy-faced lovebird *Agapornis roseicollis*

Living and breeding in flocks, these small parrots are encountered at altitudes from sea level up to 1,600m (5,250ft). They may be present in large numbers in agricultural areas when crops are ripening, a time when flocks will join together. When breeding, they may take over the abandoned nests of weaver birds, allowing them to nest in colonies. Peach-faced lovebirds have an unusual way of building their own nests: hens collect strips of nesting material and carry it back to the nest site folded and tucked into the plumage of the rump area. The nest may be sited in a wide range of localities, from cliff faces to the eaves of buildings.

Identification: Predominantly green although darker on the wings. Has a blue rump, a reddish forehead and rose-pink facial feathering that extends on to the upper breast. This rosy coloration is less pronounced in young birds, which may show traces of darker markings on their bill when fledging. Sexes alike, although pinkish coloration is reputedly paler in hens but not usually apparent. Angolan race (*A. r. catumbella*) is more lightly coloured overall.

Distribution: South-west Angola southwards to South Africa.
Size: 15cm (6in).
Habitat: Dry, wooded country.
Nest: Tree hollow or disused weaver-bird nest.
Eggs: 4–6, white.
Food: Mainly seeds, including cultivated crops such as millet and sunflower.

Masked lovebird (*Agapornis personata*): 14cm (5.5in)
Present in northern and central parts of Tanzania. The blackish head merges into a yellow collar and underparts. Wings and abdomen are green. Prominent white areas encircle the eyes. The bill is red. The legs and feet are greyish. Sexes alike.

Fischer's lovebird (*Agapornis fischeri*): 14cm (5.5in)
Found in eastern Africa – mainly in northern Tanzania. Has a reddish-orange head that becomes paler around the throat and the back of the neck, where there is a yellowish area. The underparts are light green, the wings are dark green and the rump is mauve. Has a prominent white eye ring of bare skin. The bill is red and the legs and feet are grey. Sexes are alike.

Jardine's parrot (*Poicephalus gulielmi*): 28cm (11in)
Present in central Africa from Liberia and northern Angola east to Uganda, Kenya and Tanzania. Predominantly green but with blackish feathering on the back and wings that is offset by green edging. There is a variable amount of orange plumage on the crown and the edges of the wings and thighs. The bill is greyish and the feet are pinkish. Sexes are similar, although cocks may have a more reddish-orange iris.

Vasa parrot (*Coracopsis vasa*): 50cm (20in)
Occurs on Madagascar and the Comoros, off the coast of south-eastern Africa. Predominantly brownish-black but with a greyer hue on the upperparts. Has grey undertail coverts. The bill varies seasonally from horn-coloured to grey. Sexes are alike, although cocks in breeding condition develop a prominent swelling in the region of the vent.

Ring-necked parakeet

Rose-ringed parakeet *Psittacula krameri*

Distribution: Found in a band across Africa from Senegal east to the Sudan and Uganda. Also occurs throughout Asia east to China.
Size: 40cm (16in).
Habitat: Light woodland of various types.
Nest: Tree cavity high off the ground; sometimes on a rocky ledge.
Eggs: 3–6, white.
Food: Cereals, fruit and seeds.

Identification: The African race (*P. k. krameri*) has more yellowish-green plumage, and black on the bill, than the Asiatic form (*right*), which is now established in various areas including parts of England, well outside its natural range. Hens and young birds of both sexes lack the distinctive neck collar seen in cocks, which is a combination of black and pink. Head is green.

This is the most widely distributed member of the parrot family in the world. It is naturally highly adaptable in its habits, occurring both in agricultural areas as well as cities, although it is usually observed in areas where there is woodland nearby. The increase in agriculture has meant an increased food supply in various areas of their range, and this, in turn, has helped these parrots to expand their distribution. Ring-neck parakeets fly quite high, often in small groups, and their distinctive calls carry over quite a distance, drawing attention to their presence. On mainland Africa, when their shape is silhouetted during flight showing their long tail streaming behind the body, these parakeets are unmistakable.

BARBETS

The most obvious distinguishing feature of barbets is the narrow, hair-like feathers surrounding the bill, which resemble a beard (the name "barbet" is derived from the German word for "beard"). All barbets are somewhat dumpy, compact birds, and representatives of the group occur in both the Old and New Worlds.

Levaillant's barbet

Crested barbet *Trachyphonus vaillantii*

Distribution: Most of southern Africa from Angola and Tanzania southwards, except for the south-western part of the continent.
Size: 22cm (9in).
Habitat: Open country.
Nest: Hollow chamber.
Eggs: 3–5, white.
Food: Mainly invertebrates, although also eats fruit and berries.

Although there are slight variations in the patterning of these barbets, these do not distinguish between the sexes. Levaillant's barbets are quite conspicuous birds, and are sometimes observed perching in trees or searching for food on the ground, often near termite mounds. They sometimes seek the relative security of termite mounds for breeding, tunnelling into them to create a safe nesting chamber. Their intrusion is apparently not resisted by the insects, who would usually deter most potential predators. One advantage of nesting in a termite mound is that the heat generated by their surroundings will usually keep the eggs warm when the adult birds leave their nest.

Identification: Has a reddish-orange area on the top of the head and lores, with a long black crest behind. The wings are predominantly blackish with white markings. A black band with white spots extends across the chest. The underparts are yellowish with some reddish streaks, becoming paler with fewer markings on the abdomen. The rump is yellow and red at the base. The tail feathers have white tips. The bill is a pale greenish yellow. Sexes are alike.

Double-toothed barbet

Lybius bidentatus

The unusual coloration and shape of the bill of these barbets helps to identify them in the field. The notch on the bill, which looks like a tooth, may help the birds to grasp their food. Their diet may feature more fruit than that of barbets inhabiting more open areas of country, and double-toothed barbets have a reputation for attacking ripening bananas. They are most likely to be seen in pairs than in larger groups, and pairs may breed throughout much of the year in some parts of their range. They use their strong bills to excavate a nesting site in a suitable tree by hammering at the trunk. Even so, a dead tree or branch is usually preferred as it is softer and easier for tunnelling

Identification: Predominantly black upperparts. Has a large red area on the underparts. The rump and an area on the side of the body are white. Has a blackish area around the eyes and a red wing bar. The prominent toothed bill is whitish. Sexes are alike.

Distribution: Western central Africa, from Guinea south to Angola and east to parts of Sudan, Ethiopia, Kenya and Tanzania.
Size: 23cm (9in).
Habitat: Woodland but not rainforest.
Nest: Tree hollow. Nesting chamber lined with wood chips for nesting material.
Eggs: 3–4, white.
Food: Invertebrates and fruit such as berries.

Black-collared barbet (*Lybius torquatus*):
15cm (6in)
Widely distributed across southern Africa. Distinctive crimson plumage on the face extends across the throat to the breast, with yellow beneath. The crown, nape and chest band are all black. The wings are a greenish black with some yellow evident. Sexes are alike.

D'Arnaud's barbet (*Trachyphonus darnaudii*): 17cm (7in)
Ranges in eastern Africa from Sudan, Ethiopia and Somalia west across Uganda and Kenya to south-west Tanzania. Has a black crown that is often spotted with yellow, although yellow is usually more evident on the sides of the face. Variable black markings feature on the throat and breast. The underparts are mainly a pale yellow colour. The undertail coverts are red and the upperparts are brown with white spotting. Individuals differ from each other slightly in their pattern of markings. Sexes are alike.

Pied barbet (*Lybius leucomelas*): 16cm (6in)
Present in southern Africa where it can be found in Zimbabwe, Botswana and South Africa. Has a deep red forehead, with black behind, and adjacent white stripes with some yellow suffusion extend to the back of the neck. An irregularly-shaped black area runs from below the bill down on to the chest. The remainder of the underparts are white. The wings are black apart from white markings that have a sporadic yellow suffusion. Sexes are alike.

Red-faced barbet (*Lybius rubrifacies*): 15cm (6in)
Present in southern Uganda and north-western Tanzania. An area of red plumage above the pale greyish bill extends to the sides of the face but not on to the crown or throat. The remainder of the plumage is blackish and there is a yellow edging to the wings. Sexes are alike.

Yellow-fronted tinkerbird

Pogoniulus chrysoconus

These small, relatively slim members of the barbet family will sit for long periods during the day on a well-concealed branch, uttering their monotonous-sounding call. It can be surprisingly difficult to locate them from their sound alone, however. Their lively, agile nature becomes evident when they seek food. They hover and pick insects off branches, or hop up a trunk like woodpeckers seeking grubs. They eat fruit, too, especially the berries of mistletoe and similar plants. As a result, the yellow-fronted tinkerbird helps to distribute these plants around their environment, passing seeds out in their droppings.

Distribution: Broad band across much of central Africa from Senegal east to north-west Ethiopia and Uganda.
Size: 11cm (4in).
Habitat: Savanna.
Nest: Tree hole.
Eggs: 2–3, white.
Food: Invertebrates and fruit.

Identification: Prominent yellow plumage above the upper bill, appearing almost orange in some cases, with alternating black-and-white stripes on the sides of the head. A similar, although mottled, colour combination extends over the wings, with some yellow evident on the flight feathers. The rump is sulphur yellow. Underparts are whitish with a yellowish suffusion. Legs and the long, stout bill are black. Sexes alike.

Naked-faced barbet

Gymnobucco calvus

The lack of feathering on the face of these barbets may help to prevent their plumage from becoming stained and matted by fruit juices. Young birds leave the nest with their heads almost fully feathered, but this plumage is shed and not replaced as they grow older. Social and noisy by nature, naked-faced barbets are quite conspicuous birds, encountered predominantly in lowland areas. They nest in colonies, often seeking out dead trees, where it is easier to create nesting chambers. Using their powerful bills, they excavate chambers that typically extend 23cm (9in) below the entrance. As many as 30 pairs have been reported occupying a single tree.

Identification: Predominantly brown, with significantly darker upperparts and tail. Underparts are light brown. Large, powerful bill, with beard of longer brown feathers at its base. Has bare blackish-brown skin on the head. The bare ear holes at the back of the head are clearly evident. Sexes are alike.

Distribution: From Guinea in western Africa east and south around the coastline of Africa as far as northern Angola.
Size: 18cm (7in).
Habitat: Wooded areas.
Nest: Tree hollow.
Eggs: 3, white.
Food: Invertebrates and fruit.

BEE-EATERS, KINGFISHERS AND SHRIKES

This group of birds are hunters, preying mainly on invertebrates. Although some kingfishers feed mainly on fish, those found in forested areas tend to be more insectivorous. Shrikes have a reputation for caching food in the form of so-called "larders" – they spear their prey on the sharp spines of plants, returning to retrieve the bodies when they are hungry.

Bee-eater

European bee-eater *Merops apiaster*

In spite of their name, European bee-eaters hawk a much wider range of prey in the air than simply bees. More than 300 different invertebrates have been identified in their diet, ranging from dragonflies to butterflies. They have even been known to swoop on spiders, seizing the arachnids from their webs. Although individual birds hunt on their own, European bee-eaters nest in colonies of up to eight pairs. Sandy cliffs, where they can excavate their breeding tunnels with relative ease, are favoured nesting sites. Outside the breeding season, groups roost huddled together on branches.

Identification: Whitish band above the black bill, merging into blue above the eyes. Chestnut brown extends from the top of the head down over the back, and across the wings. Golden scapulars and rump. Black band extends from the bill across the eyes. Throat is yellow, with a black band separating this area from bluish underparts. Hens have more green on wings and scapulars.

Distribution: Much of southern Europe extending into adjacent parts of Asia and into North Africa. Overwinters in western and southern Africa.
Size: 25cm (10in).
Habitat: Open country.
Nest: Tunnel in bank or cliff.
Eggs: 4–10, white.
Food: Mainly flying invertebrates.

Hoopoe

Eurasian hoopoe *Upupa epops*

The unusual appearance of these birds usually helps to identify them easily, especially as they are most likely to be observed in open country. When in flight, the broad shape of their wings is clearly visible and the tall crest is held flat over the back of the head. A hoopoe often raises its crest on landing, however. The hoopoe uses its long bill to probe for worms in the ground, or to grab prey such as lizards scurrying through the grass. Hoopoes are not especially shy of people, and pairs sometimes nest in buildings. They may often be observed dust-bathing, which keeps their plumage in good condition. The "hoo, hoo" sound of their call gives them their common name.

Identification: Mainly pale buff, although more orange on the crown and with black edging to the feathers. Alternate bands of black-and-white coloration on the wings. Long, narrow, downward-curved bill. Sexes are alike.

Above: The wing barring of the hoopoe extends under the wings, shown to best effect when in flight.

Distribution: Throughout most of Europe, although usually absent from Scandinavia and the British Isles. Overwinters in Africa south of the Equator. Also occurs in parts of North Africa and much of central Africa.
Size: 29cm (11in).
Habitat: Relatively open country.
Nest: In secluded holes.
Eggs: 5–8, whitish to yellowish olive.
Food: Mainly invertebrates, especially worms.

Kingfisher

Common kingfisher *Alcedo atthis*

These birds are surprisingly hard to spot, as they perch motionless scanning the water beneath them for fish. When it has spotted its prey, the kingfisher appears as a flash of colour as it dives. A protective membrane covers its eyes as it enters the water. Its wings provide propulsion, and having seized the fish in its bill, the bird then darts out of the water and back on to its perch with its catch. This movement happens incredibly fast, with the whole process taking little more than a mere second. The kingfisher first stuns the fish by hitting it on the perch and then swallows it head first. It regurgitates the bones and indigestible parts of its meal later.

Left: Kingfishers dive at speed into the water, aiming to catch their intended quarry unawares.

Identification: Bluish-green colour that extends over the head and wings. Back is pale blue, and a blue flash is also present on the cheeks. An area under the throat and across the back of the neck is white. Cheek patches and underparts are orange. Bill is black. In hens, the bill is reddish at the base of the lower bill.

Distribution: Occurs across most of Europe, apart from much of Scandinavia. Also present in North Africa and ranges eastwards through southern Asia to the Solomon Islands.
Size: 18cm (7in).
Habitat: Near slow-flowing water.
Nest: Tunnel excavated in sandy bank.
Eggs: 6–10, white.
Food: Small fish. Also preys on aquatic insects, molluscs and crustaceans.

Roller (European roller, *Coracias garrulus*): 32cm (12.5in)
Ranges from southern Europe east to Asia. Overwinters in western and southern Africa. Has shades of blue coloration with a greenish hue on the underparts. Has a prominent area of reddish-brown feathering over the back and wings and blue wing coverts. Powerful blackish bill. Sexes alike.

Woodland kingfisher (*Halcyon senegalensis*): 23cm (9in)
Occurs in a broad band across much of Africa south of the Sahara. Migratory in some areas. Has a greyish head that merges into a pale blue colour over the nape. The wings are blue with black areas. The rump and tail are blue. The upper bill is red and the lower bill is black. Sexes are alike.

Woodchat shrike (*Lanius senator*): 19cm (7.5in)
European distribution centres on the Mediterranean. Also occurs in western North Africa. Overwinters south in a band extending across Africa south of the Sahara. Mainly black upperparts although a chestnut area extends from the back of the head down over the neck. The underparts are white. Has a prominent white wing bar. Hens are mainly brownish, with mottled plumage and white under the chin.

Fiscal shrike (common fiscal, *Lanius collaris*): 23cm (9in)
There are two distinct populations. One ranges from sub-Saharan western Africa eastwards, the other occupies much of southern Africa. Has black upperparts with a prominent white bar. The underparts are white. Hens have rufous flanks.

Red-backed shrike

Lanius collurio

In common with many insectivorous species, the red-backed shrike migrates south each autumn, spending the winter in savanna where food is more plentiful. In some parts of this shrike's breeding range, its nests are parasitized by the common cuckoo. Unlike many such host species, however, pairs learn to recognize cuckoo eggs laid alongside their own and discard them from the nest. Cock birds often impale their prey during the breeding season, and this behaviour ensures a more constant supply of food for the chicks, although there is always a risk that scavengers will steal it.

Identification: Light grey crown. Black stripe extends from the bill across the eyes. Pinkish underparts with reddish-brown back and wings. Hens have brownish area at the front of the crown, grey behind and dark brown wings. Underparts are white with darker edging to the feathers. Brown patches behind the eyes.

Distribution: Mainland Europe, except for most of the Iberian Peninsula and northern Scandinavia. Extends into Asia, and overwinters in Africa south of the Equator.
Size: 18cm (7in).
Habitat: Open country.
Nest: Cup-shaped in the fork of a bush or tree.
Eggs: 5–9, variable coloration.
Food: Invertebrates.

SWIFTS, SWALLOWS AND MARTINS

This group of birds spend most of their lives in flight. They undertake long journeys, with European populations migrating south at the approach of winter and heading to parts of Africa, and then returning to Europe to breed in the following spring. Pairs frequently return to the same nest site that they had occupied previously – a remarkable feat of navigation after a journey covering thousands of kilometres.

Swift

Common swift *Apus apus*

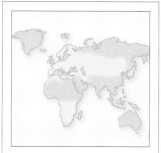

Distribution: Found virtually across the whole of Europe, also extending to North Africa and Asia. Overwinters in southern Africa.
Size: 16.5cm (6.5in).
Habitat: In the air.
Nest: Cup-shaped structure under cover.
Eggs: 2–3, white.
Food: Flying invertebrates, such as midges and moths.

Flocks of swifts are most likely to be spotted when they are uttering their distinctive screaming calls, flying low overhead in search of winged insects. At other times, they may be seen as little more than distant specks, wheeling at heights of more than 1,000m (3,300ft). Their flight pattern is quite distinctive, consisting of a series of rapid wingbeats followed by gliding into the wind. The structure of their feet does not allow them to perch, although they can cling to vertical surfaces. Swifts spend their lives in the air when they are not breeding, apparently they are able to sleep and mate in flight. If hunting conditions are unfavourable, such as a cool summer, nestling swifts respond by growing more slowly, while adults can undergo short periods of torpidity to avoid starvation.

Identification: Dark overall, with pointed wing tips and a forked tail. Pale whitish throat area. Sexes alike.

Swallow

Barn swallow *Hirundo rustica*

The return of swallows to their breeding grounds in Europe is one of the welcomed signs of spring. Although pairs return to the same nest each year, they do not migrate together. Cock birds arrive back before their partners and jealously guard the site from would-be rivals. Cocks fight with surprising ferocity if one of the birds does not back down. Although swallows sometimes use traditional nesting sites, such as caves or hollow trees, they now commonly build their nests inside buildings, such as barns, choosing a site close to the eaves. It can take as many as 1,000 trips to collect damp mud, carried back in the bill, to complete a new nest.

Identification: Chestnut forehead and throat, with dark blue head and back, and a narrow dark blue band across the chest. Wings are blackish. Underparts are white with long streamers on the tail feathers. Sexes alike.

Distribution: Throughout most of the Northern Hemisphere. European swallows overwinter in sub-Saharan Africa.
Size: 19cm (7.5in).
Habitat: Open country, close to water.
Nest: Made of mud built off the ground.
Eggs: 4–5, white with reddish and grey spotting.
Food: Flying invertebrates.

Alpine swift (*Apus melba*): 23cm (9in)
Found throughout southern Europe and North Africa. Overwinters in southern Africa. Plain brown upperparts with a black collar around the neck. Throat, chest and upper abdomen are white. Lower underparts are brown. Tail is short. Sexes alike.

Red-rumped swallow (*Hirundo daurica*): 17cm (7in)
Occurs in southern Europe, the Mediterranean and North Africa. Overwinters in sub-Saharan Africa. Dark bluish area on the head and back, separated by a wide chestnut collar. Wings are blackish. Pale chestnut rump with narrow streaking, as on the underparts. Sexes alike.

Rock martin (pale crag martin, *Hirundo fuligula*): 13cm (5in)
Occurs in Africa, apart from the central region. Also extends into south-western Asia. Brownish upperparts. Rufous-brown underparts. Those in northern areas are lighter and greyer. Sexes alike.

Plain sand martin (brown-throated sand martin, *Riparia paludicola*): 12cm (5in)
Sporadic distribution in north-western and sub-Saharan Africa. Also occurs on Madagascar. Predominantly brown overall, with a greyish-brown tinge to the throat and breast. Remainder of the underparts are white. Sexes alike.

Congo sand martin (*Riparia congica*): 11cm (4.5in)
Confined to three regions of the Congo River, hence its common name. Similar to the sand martin but the brown breast band is less defined. Sexes are alike.

House martin

Delichon urbica

The breeding habits of the house martin have changed significantly thanks to the spread of buildings in rural areas. They traditionally nested on cliffs faces, but over the past century these birds began building on the walls of houses and farm structures, as well as beneath bridges and even on street lamps, where a ready supply of nocturnal insects are attracted after dark. The nest is usually spherical and normally made of mud. The base is built first. This is followed by the sides, and on average the whole process takes up to two weeks to complete. House martins are highly social by nature, occasionally nesting in huge colonies made up of thousands of pairs where conditions are suitable. Even outside the breeding period, they will associate in large flocks of hundreds of individuals.

Identification: Dark bluish head and back with black wings. White underwing coverts, underparts and rump. Tail feathers are dark blue. Sexes alike.

Distribution: Throughout Europe, overwintering in Africa south of the Sahara Desert. Also present across much of Asia.
Size: 13cm (5in).
Habitat: Open country, close to water.
Nest: Made of mud, cup-shaped.
Eggs: 4–5, white.
Food: Flying invertebrates.

Sand martin

African sand martin; bank swallow *Riparia riparia*

In the summer months, sand martins are usually observed relatively close to lakes and other stretches of water, often swooping down to catch invertebrates over the surface. They are likely to be nesting in colonies nearby, in tunnels that they excavate on suitable sandy banks. These can extend back for up to 1m (3ft), and the nesting chamber is lined with grass, seaweed or similar material. The eggs are laid on top of a softer bed of feathers. When the young birds leave the nest, they stay in groups with other chicks, until their parents return to feed them, typically bringing about 60 invertebrates back on each visit. Parents recognize their offspring by their distinctive calls. If danger threatens, the repetitive alarm calls of the adult sand martins cause the young to rush back to the protection of the nesting tunnels.

Identification: Predominantly brown, with white plumage on the throat, separated from the white underparts by a brown band across the breast. Long flight feathers. Small black bill. Sexes alike. Immature sand martins have shorter flight feathers and are browner overall than the adults.

Distribution: Ranges across Europe and Asia to North America, overwintering in sub-Saharan Africa and South America.
Size: 11cm (4in.)
Habitat: Open country, close to water.
Nest: Holes in sandbanks.
Eggs: 3–4, white.
Food: Flying invertebrates.

PHEASANTS AND PARTRIDGES

A number of pheasants and partridges have been specially bred and released well outside their native ranges for sporting purposes, so that sightings far removed from their usual areas of distribution are not unusual. In Europe, these game birds are most likely to be observed during the winter, when there is less natural cover available and groups may be forced to forage more widely for food.

Common pheasant

Ring-necked pheasant *Phasianus colchicus*

There can be considerable variation in appearance between individuals of this species in Europe. This variation is due to hybridization between different races, resulting in the loss of distinguishing characteristics. Even odd black-feathered (melanistic) examples are not uncommon. This situation has arisen largely as a result of widespread breeding of these pheasants and their release into the wild for shooting. Their natural range is actually in Asia. They usually live in groups comprised of a cock bird with several hens. They forage for food on the ground, although they fly noisily and somewhat clumsily when disturbed and may also choose to roost off the ground.

Right: Its mottled plumage provides the common pheasant hen with good camouflage.

Identification: Prominent areas of bare red skin feature on each side of the face. They are surrounded by dark greenish, metallic plumage. Has a variable white area of plumage at the base of the neck. The remainder of the plumage is brown, with the underparts a more chestnut shade with dark blotching apparent. Hens are lighter brown overall, with darker mottling, especially on the back and wings.

Distribution: Now present throughout most of western Europe, apart from much of the Iberian Peninsula. Occurs in a band in central Asia as far east as Japan, and has also been introduced to the United States, Tasmania, Australia and New Zealand.
Size: Cock 89cm (35in); hen 62cm (24in).
Habitat: Lightly wooded areas.
Nest: Scrape on the ground.
Eggs: 7–15, olive brown.
Food: Plant matter, such as seeds, berries and young shoots, and invertebrates.

Red-legged partridge

Alectoris rufa

The adaptable nature of these partridges is reflected by the fact that the species is now breeding well outside its natural range, having first been brought to England as long ago as the late 1600s for sporting purposes. During the 20th century, however, the chukar partridge, which hybridizes with the red-legged variety, was introduced to the British Isles. Today it can be difficult to determine whether the partridges sighted are pure or cross-bred red-legged individuals, even in their natural range, thanks to their similarity in appearance to chukars. Red-legged partidges form individual pairs when breeding. The cock bird chooses, then prepares, the nest site.

Identification: The prominent black collar with similar streaking extending back around the neck helps to identify this species. Black stripe extends across the eye with narrow white band above and white area extending down around the throat. Bluish-grey area above the bill, and bluish-grey on the breast and barred flanks. Brownish abdomen. Hens smaller and lack tarsal spur on the legs.

Distribution: Found naturally in Europe from the Iberian Peninsula to Italy. Introduced to the rest of Europe.
Size: 38cm (15in).
Habitat: Open countryside.
Nest: Scrape on the ground.
Eggs: 9–12, pale yellowish brown with dark spotting.
Food: Plant matter and some invertebrates.

Rock partridge

Alectoris graeca

Distribution: Central southern Europe, from France east to Italy, Greece and the former Yugoslavia. Also present on Sicily.
Size: 36cm (14in).
Habitat: Rocky alpine areas.
Nest: Scrape on the ground.
Eggs: 8–14, yellowish brown with some darker spotting.
Food: Plant matter and some invertebrates.

The name of these partridges stems from the fact that they are often observed on rocky slopes, ranging to altitudes as high as 2,700m (8,850ft) in Italy. They often move down to lower levels when snow collects on the slopes in the winter, and they avoid north-facing slopes. Throughout the year, rock partridges are rarely sighted far from water. They are most likely to be observed in flocks, although their coloration provides excellent camouflage when they are on the ground. When flushed, their flight is quite low and fast, and they will dip down into nearby cover again as soon as they are out of apparent danger. Rock partridges nest as individual pairs, and their chicks are fully grown by three months old.

Identification: Grey crown with black stripe running from around the red bill across the eye and down on to the chest, which has bordering white feathering. Underparts are greyish-blue, becoming fawn on the underparts, with black-and-white barring on the flanks. Brownish suffusion over the back. Sexes are alike.

Helmeted guineafowl

Numida meleagris

There is considerable diversity in the appearance of these guineafowl through their wide range. In the past, taxonomists have recognized more than 30 different races, but this figure has been whittled down to approximately nine today. The shape of the casque and wattles, as well as the depth of the blue coloration on the sides of the head, help to distinguish the various subspecies. Helmeted guineafowl prey readily on invertebrates, even to the extent of picking off ticks from warthogs. When searching for seeds or other food on the ground, they scratch around using their powerful toes. The young are able to fly just 14 days after hatching, and family groups link up with the main flock again after a month or so.

Distribution: Much of Africa south of the Sahara, apart from areas of central Africa. Introduced elsewhere, including Saudi Arabia and the Caribbean.
Size: 53–63cm (21–25in).
Habitat: Open country, especially savanna.
Nest: Scrape on the ground, often hidden in long grass.
Eggs: 6–12, creamy buff with brown-and-white speckling.
Food: Plant matter and invertebrates.

Identification: Distinctive horn-coloured casque on the top of the head, often with adjoining area of red skin, and blue areas on the sides of the face extending down the neck. Traces of fine down feathering may be visible, but head is largely bare. Plumage is dark overall broken with variable white spots. Sexes similar but hens are smaller than cocks.

Chukar partridge (*Alectoris chukar*):
35cm (14in)
Found in southern Europe eastwards to Asia. Introduced to the British Isles and elsewhere. Very similar to the rock partridge but has a cream (rather than white) area on the sides of the face and chest, a broader white stripe above the eyes, and black is present only on the side of the lower mandible rather than the whole bill. Numerous races recognized through its wide range. Hens lack the tarsal swelling of cocks, and their head patterning is less colourful.

Grey partridge (*Perdix perdix*):
32cm (12.5in)
Occurs in a broad band across central Europe, from Ireland eastwards to Asia. Orange-brown face, with stripe extending further back on the sides of the head. Crown, neck and much of the underparts are greyish with dark edging to the plumage. The prominent dark brown feathering on the belly is absent or reduced in size in hens. The flanks are barred with brown. Wings are brown with black speckling. Tail is reddish brown.

Barbary partridge (*Alectoris barbara*):
35cm (14in)
Natural range is in North Africa. Introduced to southern Spain and also present on Sardinia. Dark stripe on the crow, with a greyish-white area beneath and a lighter fawn stripe extending across the eyes. The remainder of the head and throat area are greyish white. Has a reddish-brown border to the bib with black-and-white speckling behind. The chest is otherwise greyish and the abdomen is fawn. The back and wings are greyish with a fawn suffusion. Has brown and black markings on the flanks on a whitish background. Sexes are alike.

QUAILS AND BUSTARDS

This group of birds inhabit open areas of country, relying mainly on their often cryptic coloration to conceal their presence. The distribution of grouse extends to the frozen wastelands of the tundra zone in the far north. They are adapted to living on the ground here, and also have plumage that extends right down over the toes to restrict heat loss and guard against frostbite.

Common quail

Eurasian migratory quail *Coturnix coturnix*

Although these relatively small quails often inhabit agricultural areas, they are hard to spot thanks to their shy natures and the effective camouflage provided by their plumage. Common quails prefer to remain concealed, but take to the wing when necessary, when they are both agile and fast. Their wings appear relatively large when flying, reflecting the fact that these small birds may fly long distances each year. There is a distinction between the resident African population and migratory birds, with the latter being slightly larger in size and not as rufous in coloration. Throughout their range, these quails tend to occur in areas of grassland, as this vegetation provides them with natural cover.

Identification: A pale stripe runs above the eye and a thinner, narrower black stripe runs beneath. There is a small white area faintly bordered by black on the upper chest. The top of the head and back are dark brown. The remainder of the underparts are fawn, becoming paler on the abdomen. Hens lack the white patch, have mottled plumage and are duller in their overall colouration. Young common quail look very similar to the adult hens, but can be distinguished by the absence of stripes on the lower part of their cheeks and the absence of barring on their flanks.

Distribution: Occurs in Europe in summer, wintering in Africa south of the Sahara. Also resident in North Africa.
Size: 18cm (7in).
Habitat: Open country.
Nest: Grass-lined scrape on the ground.
Eggs: 5–13, buff with darker markings.
Food: Seeds and some invertebrates.

Great bustard

Otis tarda

These massive birds have declined greatly in number over recent years owing to the combination of hunting and habitat change. They still flourish in undisturbed areas, where they are seen in groups throughout the year. The display of the cock is an amazing sight as he bends forwards, raising his wings and inflating his throat sac. His head disappears from view, creating what has been likened to a foam bath. In spite of their size, great bustards are quiet birds by nature, uttering a short call resembling a bark only if alarmed. Although adults will hunt voles, invertebrates are favoured for rearing chicks, which is accomplished by the hen alone.

Identification: Grey head and neck, with a rufous area at the base. Black and chestnut markings on the wings, with prominent white areas. Underparts and tips of tail feathers are also white. Hens have more extensive but paler rufous coloration on the neck, and less white on the wings.

Distribution: Scattered throughout the Iberian Peninsula. Also present in parts of central Europe and ranges eastwards into Asia.
Size: Cock 105cm (41in); hen 75cm (29.5in).
Habitat: Open steppes and farmland.
Nest: Flattened area of vegetation.
Eggs: 2–4, greenish or olive brown.
Food: Plant matter, invertebrates and small mammals.

Willow grouse (red grouse, *Lagopus lagopus*): 35–43cm (14–17in)
Has a circumpolar distribution, which includes northern areas of the British Isles (where the race concerned is called red grouse) and Scandinavia. Has a brownish head and upperparts, and white underparts. Becomes pure white during the winter. Hens are similar but have much more speckled upperparts, but also become pure white in winter.

Black grouse (Eurasian black grouse, *Tetrao tetrix*): Cock 58cm (23in); hen 45cm (18cm)
Present in Scotland and northern England. Extends from Belgium north to Scandinavia and east across northern Asia. Also occurs in the Alpine region. Predominantly jet black, with scarlet combs above the eyes. Odd white areas form a wing bar and undertail coverts and create spotting in the shoulder area. The tail feathers are decidedly curved. The hen is predominantly brown speckled with black barring, and has a narrow white wing bar.

Hazel grouse (*Bonasa bonasia*): 40cm (16in)
Occurs in north-eastern France, Belgium and Germany north to Scandinavia and eastwards across Asia. Has a distinctive-looking solid black throat patch outlined in white and a tall crest. The back, vent and legs are greyish. Darker abdominal markings are highlighted on a white background. Rufous patches appear the sides of the chest. Hens have a speckled throat patch and a smaller crest.

Caucasian black grouse (*Tetrao mlokosiewiczi*): 55cm (22in)
Present in parts of Turkey and the Caucasian Mountains. Almost entirely black, apart from a small white patch in the shoulder area of each wing and a prominent red stripe above each eye. Relatively long, slightly curved tail. Hens are greyish brown overall, with relatively fine barring over the body and dark ear coverts.

Capercaillie
Western capercaillie *Tetrao urogallus*

Cocks are similar in some respects to New World turkeys, adopting a very similar display pose with their tail feathers fanned out in a circle. They display communally to hens at sites known as leks. After mating with her chosen partner, the hen nests and rears the young by herself. The weather in the critical post-hatching period has a major impact on the survival rate of the chicks. In wet springs, many become fatally chilled. Hens are about a third of the weight of cocks. Both sexes have strong, hooked bills, which enable them to nip off pieces of tough vegetation, such as Scots pine shoots, with relative ease, allowing them to survive even when there is snow covering the ground.

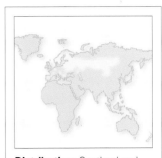

Distribution: Scotland and mountainous areas in western Europe. Also ranges through much of Scandinavia and northern Asia.
Size: 80–115cm (31–45in).
Habitat: Areas with coniferous and deciduous trees.
Nest: Shallow scrape on the ground.
Eggs: 6–10, yellow with light brown blotches.
Food: Mainly buds and shoots.

Left: The male capercaillie uses its tail feathers to form a fan shape when displaying.

Identification: Greyish-black head with an obvious red stripe above each eye. Green area on the chest, with chestnut wings. Rump and tail are blackish. Underparts are variable, ranging from predominantly white to black. Legs are covered with brown feathers, toes are exposed. Hens have an orangish patch on the sides of the face and chest, brown mottled upperparts and whiter underparts.

LARKS, PIPITS, WAGTAILS AND FLYCATCHERS

Although the coloration of this group of birds tends to be relatively subdued, some members such as the skylark are well known for their song. They are dependent on invertebrates for a major part of their diet, so a number of the species occurring in Europe, especially flycatchers, migrate further south in the autumn each year to obtain a more dependable food supply during the winter.

Common skylark

Alauda arvensis

The coloration and patterning of the skylark help it to remain hidden on the ground, where it sometimes freezes to escape detection. If disturbed at close quarters, however, it takes off almost vertically. Skylarks are unusual in that they reveal their presence readily by singing. They engage in what are described as song flights – fluttering their wings, they rise slowly through the air to a height of typically 100m (330ft) or so. The distinctive rounded song of the skylark can be heard through most of the year, even in the depths of winter. During the breeding period in the spring and summer, a sitting hen may draw attention away from her nest site by feigning injury, dragging one wing along the ground and taking off only as a last resort.

Above: The skylark's nest is well concealed on the ground.

Identification: Greyish-brown plumage over the back and wings, with speckling becoming paler on the flanks. Underparts are mainly white. Whitish stripe extends back from the eyes, and ear coverts are greyish. Short crest on the crown, although it is not always visible. Hens are similar but lack the crest.

Distribution: Resident throughout much of western Europe from Denmark southwards. Also occurs in North Africa. Breeding range extends further north to Scandinavia and eastwards to Asia.
Size: 18cm (7in).
Habitat: Open countryside, especially farmland.
Nest: On the ground hidden in grass.
Eggs: 3–5, greyish, darkly spotted eggs.
Food: Plant matter and invertebrates.

Grey wagtail

Motacilla cinerea

Fast-flowing streams and similar stretches of water are areas where grey wagtails are most likely to be observed, as they dart fearlessly across rocks in search of invertebrates. They live in pairs and construct their cup-shaped nest in a well-concealed locality, usually close to water and sometimes in among the roots of a tree or an ivy-clad wall. These wagtails have benefited from some changes in their environment, taking advantage of millstreams and adjacent buildings to expand their area of distribution, but they can still be forced to leave their territory in search of food during severe winters, especially if the water freezes.

Identification: Grey head and wings, with a narrow white band with black beneath running across the eyes. White border to the black bib on the throat. Underparts are yellow, which is brightest on the chest and at the base of the tail. Sexes similar but hens have a grey or even greyish-white bib and much whiter underparts. Darker feathering disappears from the throat in winter.

Distribution: Resident throughout most of western Europe, except Scandinavia. Also present in North Africa and Asia, where the population tends to be more migratory.
Size: 20cm (8in).
Habitat: Near flowing water.
Nest: In rock crevices and similar sites.
Eggs: 4–6, buff with greyish, marbled markings.
Food: Invertebrates.

Pied wagtail

Motacilla alba

These lively birds have adapted to changes in their environment, moving from coastal areas and marshland into farmland. Today they can even often be observed hunting on and beside roads. Pied wagtails are not especially shy birds, and the movements of their tail feathers, which give them their common name, strike an unmistakable jaunty pose. The race that breeds in the British Isles is different from that observed elsewhere in Europe as cocks have black plumage on their backs during the summer. This area turns to grey for the rest of the year. The mainland European form is often described as the white wagtail as these birds have a greyish back for the whole year.

Identification: Variable through range. Prominent white area on the head with a black crown and nape. A black area extends from the throat down on to the chest. The rest of the underparts are white. The back is grey or black depending on where the wagtail is from. Hens have more ashy-grey backs, which form a smudged border with the black feathering above.

Distribution: Resident throughout western Europe and in western North Africa, with the winter distribution there more widespread. Seen in Scandinavia and Iceland only during the summer.
Size: 19cm (7.5in).
Habitat: Open areas.
Nest: Concealed, sometimes in walls.
Eggs: 5–6, whitish with grey markings.
Food: Invertebrates.

Greater short-toed lark (*Calandrella brachydactyla*): 16cm (6in)
Breeds mainly in southern Europe and North Africa although sometimes seen as far north as the British Isles. Overwinters in Africa and the Middle East. Has largely unmarked white underparts. A dark patch of feathering features on each side of the throat. Has a dark wing bar although wings are otherwise brownish and streaked. The eye stripes are white, and the ear coverts are a darker brownish colour. Sexes are alike.

Bar-tailed desert lark (*Ammomanes cincturus*): 14cm (5.5in)
Extends from north-western Africa into parts of the Middle East. Pale sandy-brown overall, with brownish wings, darker at the tips of the flight feathers. Has a black bar across the tail feathers, which is clearly visible in flight. Sexes are alike.

Meadow pipit (*Anthus pratensis*): 15cm (6in)
Resident in the British Isles and neighbouring parts of western Europe east to Denmark. Individuals from more northerly and easterly areas overwinter around the Mediterranean. Brownish head and wings with darker markings. Dark streaking on the breast and flanks, which are a darker shade of buff. Underparts become whiter in the summer. Sexes are alike.

Collared flycatcher (*Ficedula albicollis*): 13cm (5in)
Occurs as a summertime breeding visitor in central eastern parts of Europe, overwintering in Africa. Similar to the pied flycatcher, but cocks are usually identified by the presence of a white collar encircling the neck and a white area on the rump. Hens have a distinct white patch on the edge of the wings and greyer upperparts.

Pied flycatcher

Ficedula hypoleuca

These flycatchers hawk invertebrates in flight, as well as catching slower-moving prey such as caterpillars by plucking them off vegetation. They are frequently seen in oak woodlands in Europe during the summer, but may range north to the taiga, where mosquitoes hatching in pools of water during the brief summer provide an almost constant supply of food. Pied flycatchers are closely related to collared flycatchers and may sometimes hybridize with them. It is usually possible to identify the male offspring of these pairings by the narrow area of black plumage evident on the nape of the neck.

Distribution: Summer visitor to Europe, breeding as far north as Scandinavia. Overwinters in Africa.
Size: 13cm (5in).
Habitat: Areas in which insects are common.
Nest: Hole in a tree.
Eggs: 5–9, pale blue.
Food: Invertebrates.

Identification: Plumage in summer is a combination of black and white, with white patches above the bill and on the wings. Underparts are white and the remainder of the plumage is black. Hens also have whitish underparts, with a white area on the wing, while the upperparts are brownish. Cocks during winter resemble adult hens, but retain blackish wing and uppertail coverts.

PIGEONS AND DOVES

The columbiforms have adapted well to living in close association with people, although their presence is not always welcomed. Large flocks of feral pigeons can cause serious damage to buildings in urban areas, not just with their droppings but also by pecking at the mortar, which is a source of calcium. Their adaptable nature is further reflected by the fact that they will often breed throughout much of the year.

Rock dove

Columba livia

Although true rock doves have a localized range, their descendants – feral pigeons – are a very common sight even in large capital cities. In the past, monastic communities kept and bred rock doves, and the young doves, known as squabs, were highly valued as a source of meat. Inevitably, some birds escaped from their dovecotes, and the offspring of these birds, which reverted to the wild, gave rise to today's feral pigeons. Colour mutations have also occurred, and apart from the so-called "blue" form, there are now red and even mainly white individuals on city streets today, scavenging whatever they can from our leftovers.

Identification: Dark bluish-grey head, slight green iridescence on the neck, with light grey wings and two characteristic black bars across each wing. Feral pigeons often have longer wings than rock doves. Reddish-purple coloration on the sides of the upper chest. Remainder of the plumage is grey with a black band at the tip of the tail feathers. Sexes alike.

Above: The rock dove nests on loose twigs.

Distribution: Occurs naturally in northern areas of Scotland and nearby islands, and in western Ireland. Also found around the Mediterranean. Distribution of the feral pigeon extends throughout Europe and southern Africa, as well as to other continents.
Size: 35cm (14in).
Habitat: Originally cliffs and mountainous areas.
Nest: Loose pile of twigs or similar material.
Eggs: 2, white.
Food: Mainly seeds.

Wood pigeon

Columba palumbus

Distribution: Occurs throughout virtually all of western Europe, ranging eastwards into Asia and also present in north-western Africa.
Size: 43cm (17in).
Habitat: Areas with tall trees.
Nest: Platform of twigs.
Eggs: 2, white.
Food: Seeds, plant matter and invertebrates.

Identification: Grey head, with a reflective metallic-green area at the nape of the neck and characteristic white patches on the sides. Bill is reddish at the base, becoming yellow towards the top. Purplish breast becoming paler on the underparts. Tip of tail is black. White edging to the wings most evident in flight, forming a distinct band. Sexes alike.

These pigeons can be significant agricultural pests in areas of arable farming. Even in towns, they will frequent parks where there are established stands of trees, and descend into nearby gardens and allotments to raid growing crops. On occasion, however, they also eat potential crop pests such as snails. Pairs sometimes nest on buildings, but they prefer a suitable tree fork. Their calls are surprisingly loud and are often uttered soon after dawn. Outside the breeding season, these birds congregate in larger numbers. Their relatively large size means that they appear quite clumsy when taking off if danger threatens.

Collared dove

Streptopelia decaocto

The westerly spread of these doves during the second half of the 20th century was one of the most dramatic examples of the changing patterns of distribution among bird species. In this case, the triggers for the distribution change are unclear. Collared doves had been recorded in Hungary in the 1930s, and they moved rapidly over the next decade across Germany and Austria to France, and also headed north to Denmark and the Netherlands. The species was first sighted in eastern England during 1952, and a pair bred there three years later. The earliest Irish record was reported in 1959, and by the mid-1960s the collared dove had colonized almost all of the UK. No other bird species has spread naturally so far and so rapidly in recent times, to the extent that the collared dove's range now extends right across Europe and Asia.

Identification: Pale greyish-fawn with a narrow black half-collar around the back of the neck. Dark flight feathers with white edging along the leading edge of the wing. White tips to tail feathers visible when spread. Depth of individual coloration can vary. Sexes are alike.

Above: The collared dove is a frequent visitor to towns and will happily build its nest on the roof tops.

Distribution: Across Europe, apart from the far north of Scandinavia and the Alps, eastwards to Asia. More localized on the Iberian Peninsula and in North Africa particularly.
Size: 34cm (13in).
Habitat: Parks and gardens.
Nest: Platform of twigs.
Eggs: 2, white.
Food: Seeds and some plant matter.

Laughing dove

Streptopelia senegalensis

These highly adaptable doves are often seen in urban habitats, particularly in areas where they are expanding their range. In Australia, for example, bird-table offerings have afforded them a constant supply of suitable food, allowing them to become established here well away from their natural range. In North Africa, they are frequently encountered near oases, which has led to them becoming known as palm doves. Their fast breeding cycle, with chicks hatching and leaving the nest within a month of the eggs being laid, means that they can increase their numbers rapidly under favourable conditions. Pairs may attempt to breed throughout most of the year, rather than having a prescribed breeding period like many bird species, particularly those occurring outside the tropics.

Distribution: Widely distributed in Africa, both north and south of the Sahara Desert, although absent from western central parts. Also extends throughout the Middle East to Asia. Introduced to Western Australia.
Size: 26cm (10in).
Habitat: Acacia woodland, oases and open country.
Nest: Loose platform of twigs.
Eggs: 2, white.
Food: Mainly seeds and invertebrates.

Identification: Reddish brown, with brown and black speckled collar under the neck. Grey bar on the leading edge of the wing. Pale underparts. Has a long, relatively dark tail. Sexes are alike.

Stock pigeon (stock dove, *Columba oenas*): 32cm (12.5in)
Throughout Europe, but absent from much of Scotland, northern Scandinavia and most of the mountainous central region. Range does extend to north-western Africa and east to Asia. Grey head with green iridescence on the neck. Wings are dark grey with black markings and a black band across the tips of the tail feathers. Pale grey rump and lower underparts. The chest is pinkish grey.

European turtle dove (*Streptopelia turtur*): 27cm (10.5in)
Much of Europe but not common in Ireland, Scotland or Scandinavia. Present in North Africa. More brightly coloured on the wings than its East Asian cousin, having orange-brown feathers with darker centres. Black-and-white barring on the sides of the neck. Head is greyish. Underparts are pale with a slight pinkish hue. White edge to the tail feathers.

Cape dove (Namaqua dove, *Oena capensis*): 26cm (10in)
Found in Africa south of the Sahara, including Madagascar. Also present in southern Israel and Arabia. Black area from the forehead down on to the chest, with bluish grey behind. Long, narrow tail. Dark flight feathers and black markings on the wings, with rufous underwing areas. Upperparts are light grey, whiter on the underparts. Hens lack the black area on the face, displaying only a narrow stripe extending from the bill to the eye.

SPARROWS, WEAVERS AND WHYDAHS

Various members of this group of birds have benefited from the impact of human changes to the environment. These changes have led not only to a greater availability of food, but also to a corresponding increase in nesting sites in urban areas. These birds tend to live in flocks, and in some cases cock birds are transformed by a nuptial moult at the start of the breeding season.

House sparrow

Passer domesticus

A common sight on bird tables and in city parks, house sparrows have adapted to living closely alongside people, even to the extent of nesting under roofs in buildings. These sparrows form loose flocks, with larger numbers congregating where food is readily available. They spend much of their time on the ground, hopping along and ever watchful for passing predators such as cats. It is not uncommon for them to construct nests during the winter time, which serve as communal roosts rather than being used for breeding. The bills of cock birds turn black at the start of the nesting period in the spring. During this time, several males often court a single female in what has become known as a "sparrows' wedding". In more rural areas, these sparrows will sometimes nest in tree hollows, and even construct domed nests on occasion.

Identification: Rufous-brown head with a grey area on top. A black stripe runs across the eyes and a broad black bib runs down over the chest. Has a whitish area under the tail. The ear coverts and the entire underparts are greyish. Hens are a duller shade of brown with a pale stripe behind each eye and a fawn bar on each wing.

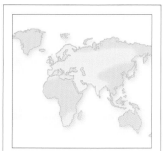

Distribution: Occurs throughout virtually all of Europe and eastwards into Asia. Also present in North and south-east Africa.
Size: 15cm (6in).
Habitat: Urban and more rural areas.
Nest: Buildings and tree hollows.
Eggs: 3–6, whitish with darker markings.
Food: Seeds and invertebrates, which are especially sought during the breeding season.

Orange weaver

Red bishop *Euplectes orix*

The stocky bills of these weavers not only assist them in cracking the seeds that form the basis of their diet, but also make highly effective needles, allowing them to weave their elaborate nests effectively. This is a learned skill, which improves with practice, and young cocks, with their clumsily constructed nests, are far less likely to attract mates than experienced males. Cocks are polygamous, with each mature male mating with several hens and providing each with a nesting site, although he will take no direct role in hatching the eggs or rearing the chicks.

Above: By weaving their nests, orange weavers can site them in areas where they are more likely to be out of reach of predators.

Distribution: South of the Sahara, extending eastwards to Ethiopia and south to southern Africa.
Size: 13cm (5in).
Habitat: Grasslands.
Nest: Woven from grasses.
Eggs: 3–4, pale blue.
Food: Seeds, vegetation and some invertebrates.

Identification: Cocks in breeding colour have a ruff of orangish red around the head, with a black face, lower breast and upper abdomen. Darker blackish-red area over the mantle, Lower back and abdomen are orangish-red. Flight feathers are brown. Hen and out-of-colour cock (left) have brownish-black streaking on the upperparts, with a pale yellowish stripe above each eye, buff underparts and light streaking on the sides of the breast.

Pintailed whydah

Vidua macroura

The finery and display of the cock bird attracts a harem of hens during the breeding period. After mating, however, the female pintailed whydah lays individual eggs in the nests of waxbills, rather than constructing her own. As many as 19 different species have been recorded as playing host to young whydahs, and this species ranks among the most adaptable of all birds displaying parasitic breeding behaviour. Unlike the common cuckoo, however, young whydahs do not kill their fellow nestlings but are reared alongside them, even mimicking their mouth markings on hatching. This fools the hosts into believing that the whydah is one of their own.

Identification: Breeding cocks have a black cap, and white collar, sides of the face and underparts. Remainder of the upperparts is black, apart from white wing bars and very long tail plumes. Hens and out-of-colour cocks have black stripes running from the sides of the bill up to the eyes, and a black area on the crown. Speckling is evident over the back and wings. Underparts are a lighter shade of fawn.

Distribution: Occurs widely across Africa south of the Sahara Desert.
Size: 11cm (4in) excluding male's tail plumes, which reach 25cm (10in).
Habitat: Open country.
Nest: Parasitizes those of other species, mainly waxbills.
Eggs: 3, whitish.
Food: Seeds and some invertebrates.

Tree sparrow (*Passer montanus*): 14cm (5.5in)
Present in all mainland Europe apart from northern Scandinavia, western England, northern Scotland and central Ireland. The top of the head is reddish-brown and there is a black bib beneath the bill. A white area on the cheeks below the eyes extends back around the neck and is broken by central black patches. Grey chest. The wings are light brown and black, broken by a white wing bar edged by black. Sexes are alike.

Red-collared whydah (*Euplectes ardens*): 13cm (5in)
Ranges in eastern and central Africa. Breeding males are black, apart from a scarlet, crescent-shaped area on the upper breast. Long tail feathers add 15cm (6in) to their overall length. Hens and out-of-colour cocks have black and brown streaking on their upperparts and buff coloration on their underparts.

Indigo bird (*Vidua chalybeata*): 13cm (5in)
Ranges in western Africa from Mauritania to Chad and Nigeria. Crown has a pale streak with a darker border. Breeding cocks have bluish-black plumage, and reddish bill, legs and feet. Hens and out-of-colour cocks have dark and light brown streaking on the upperparts and buff-white underparts.

Napoleon weaver (Golden bishop, *Euplectes afer*): 13cm (5in)
Ranges in western Africa from Senegal to Chad, the Central African Republic and the Congo. Has a yellow crown and back with a blackish hue on the collar, a yellow breast and black abdomen. The wings and tail are brownish black. There is streaking on the upper-parts. Buff underparts with darker streaking. Breeding cocks have a black mask and throat. Hens and out-of-colour cocks have a black head.

Red-billed weaver

Black-faced dioch; red-billed quelea *Quelea quelea*

This weaver is considered to be the most numerous bird in the world, with the total population estimated at ten billion individuals. It lives in large flocks that can inflict massive damage on ripening crops of millet and other seeds. To reflect this, red-billed weavers are often called feathered locusts. These birds breed communally. Nests are built closely together in thorn trees, and these help to deter potential predators and also serve as fixing points for the nests.

Distribution: Ranges widely across Africa south of the Sahara Desert, eastwards to Sudan and Ethiopia and south to northern South Africa and Angola.
Size: 13cm (5in).
Habitat: Often close to reed beds.
Nest: Made of grasses.
Eggs: 2–4, pale blue.
Food: Seeds and invertebrates.

Identification: Both sexes have brown and black streaked plumage outside the nesting season. Cocks in breeding colour have a black mask, with pinkish plumage on the head extending across the underparts. Dark brown and black wings. Tail feathers are dark.

WRENS, TITS, NUTHATCHES AND WARBLERS

These relatively small birds are most likely to be spotted in gardens during the winter months, when the absence of leaves on trees makes them more conspicuous. Tits, in particular, are also frequent visitors to bird feeders and tables during colder weather. They can prove to be very resourceful when seeking food, clearly displaying their skill in aerobatics as they dart about and hang upside down to feed.

Wren

Troglodytes troglodytes

Although the wren's small size makes these tiny birds difficult to spot, their song is loud for their size and will betray their presence. Wrens are often found in areas where there is plenty of cover, such as ivy-clad walls, where they hunt for food, scurrying under the vegetation in search of spiders and similar prey. During the winter, when their small size could make them vulnerable to hypothermia, these wrens huddle together in roosts overnight to keep warm. In the spring, the hen chooses one of several nests that the male has constructed, lining it with feathers to form a soft base for her eggs. Wrens are surprisingly common, although not always conspicuous, with the British population alone made up of an estimated ten million birds. Populations are often badly affected by prolonged spells of severe weather.

Identification: Reddish-brown back and wings with barring visible. Lighter brown underparts and a narrow eye stripe. Short tail, often held vertically, which is greyish on its underside. Bill is long and relatively narrow. Sexes alike.

Distribution: Resident throughout Europe, apart from Scandinavia and neighbouring parts of Russia during the winter. Wrens in Europe move south in the winter. Present in North Africa.
Size: 10cm (4in).
Habitat: Overgrown gardens and woodland.
Nest: Ball-shaped.
Eggs: 5–6, white with reddish-brown markings.
Food: Mainly invertebrates.

Eurasian nuthatch

Sitta europaea

The relatively large, strong feet and powerful claws of the Eurasian nuthatch give a hint as to the behaviour of these birds. They are adept at scampering up and down tree trunks, hunting for invertebrates, which they extract with their narrow bills. Their compact and powerful beak also enables these birds to feed easily on nuts, which they first wedge into a suitable crevice in the bark. Nuthatches then hammer at the shell, breaking it open so they can extract the kernel. They also store nuts, which they can use when other food is in short supply. The bill is also a useful tool to help the birds plaster over the entrance to their nest hole in the spring. The small opening just allows the birds to squeeze in, helping to protect them from predators. These nuthatches are most likely to be encountered in areas with broad-leafed trees, as these provide food such as acorns and hazelnuts.

Distribution: Found throughout most of Europe, apart from Ireland, northern England, Scotland and much of Scandinavia. Occurs in North Africa opposite the Strait of Gibraltar.
Size: 14cm (5.5in).
Habitat: Gardens and parks with mature trees.
Nest: In a secluded spot.
Eggs: 6–9, white with heavy reddish-brown speckling.
Food: Invertebrates and seeds.

Identification: Bluish-grey upperparts from head to tail, with a black stripe running across the eyes. Underparts vary in colour, depending on the race, from white through to a rusty shade of buff. Dark reddish-brown vent area, more brightly coloured in cocks.

Blue tit

Parus caeruleus

Distribution: Throughout Europe except the far north of Scandinavia. Also present in north-western Africa.
Size: 12cm (5in).
Habitat: Wooded areas in parks and gardens.
Nest: Tree holes.
Eggs: 7–16, white with reddish-brown markings.
Food: Invertebrates, seeds and nuts.

A common visitor to bird tables, blue tits are lively, active birds by nature, and are welcomed by gardeners because they eat aphids. Their small size allows them to hop up the stems of thin plants and, hanging upside down, seek these pests under leaves. Blue tits are well adapted to garden life and readily adopt nest boxes supplied for them. Their young leave the nest before they are able to fly properly, and are vulnerable to predators such as cats at this time. Those that do survive the critical early weeks can be easily distinguished by the presence of yellow rather than white cheek patches.

Identification: Has a distinctive area of blue on the crown, edged with white, and narrow black stripe running across eyes. Cheeks are white. Underparts are yellowish. The back is a greyish-green. There is a whitish bar across the top of the blue wings. The tail is also blue. Sexes similar but hens duller.

Willow warbler

Phylloscopus trochilus

Distribution: Occurs in the summer from the British Isles right across northern Europe. Overwinters in Africa.
Size: 12cm (5in).
Habitat: Wooded areas.
Nest: Domed, built on the ground.
Eggs: 6–7, pale pink with reddish spotting.
Food: Small invertebrates.

The subdued coloration of these small birds is so effective that, in spite of being one of Europe's most common bird species, the willow warbler is relatively inconspicuous. They are quite difficult to observe in the wooded areas that they frequent, although their song, which heralds their arrival in the spring, will betray their presence. In the British Isles, the willow warbler is the most numerous warbler; the population is estimated to comprise three million pairs. These warblers are usually resident in Europe between April and September. The nest is well hidden in vegetation and features a low entry point. In late summer, willow warblers are often observed in loose association with various tits, before heading off to their wintering grounds.

Identification: Greyish-green upperparts, with a pale yellowish streak running across the eyes. Pale yellow throat and chest, with whitish underparts. The yellow plumage is much whiter in birds from more northern areas.

Long-tailed tit (*Aegithalos caudatus*): 15cm (6in)
Occurs throughout most of Europe, except for much of northern Scandinavia. Distinctive narrow, long tail feathers, up to 9cm (3.5in) long. Head predominantly white, with a variable black streak above the eyes. Reddish-brown patches on the upper part of the wings and the flanks. Back and wings are otherwise black.

Great tit (*Parus major*): 15cm (6in)
Present throughout Europe and extends to north-western Africa. Also occurs in eastern Asia. Prominent black head with white patches on the cheeks. Black stripe extending from the throat down the midline of the underparts, which is far more prominent in cocks than hens. The rest of the underparts are yellow. Greyish-green back, with a white wing bar and blue hues.

Coal tit (*Parus ater*): 11cm (4in)
Range extends throughout most of Europe, apart from the far north of Scandinavia. Also present in north-western Africa. Coal-black markings on the head, with a white area on the nape and cheeks. Brownish-white underparts. Olive-grey wings with white markings. North African race has yellow rather than white markings.

Blackcap warbler (*Sylvia atricapilla*): 15cm (6in)
Ranges over most of Europe in the summer, apart from northern Scandinavia. Moves south in winter and has a resident population restricted largely to southern parts of the British Isles (including Ireland), France, the Iberian Peninsula and Italy. Also resident in north-western Africa. Jet black area on the crown, extending just above the eye and bordered by grey above the bill. Remainder of the head and breast is greyish. Has white plumage under the throat. Back, wings and underparts are olive grey. Sexes alike. Young birds have a reddish brown cap.

FINCHES

By feeding mainly on seeds, but adopting different feeding strategies, finch species can exploit a wide variety of food sources without competing with each other. At one extreme, goldfinches, for example, can probe for and eat small seeds, whereas the stout-billed hawfinch can crack cherry seeds, exerting a force equivalent to 50kg (110lb) to reach the kernel within.

Chaffinch

Fringilla coelebs

The behaviour of the chaffinch changes significantly during the year. These birds can be seen in groups during the winter, but at the onset of spring, and the breeding season, cock birds become very territorial, driving away any rivals. While resident chaffinches remain in gardens and similar settings throughout the year, large groups of migrants seeking refuge from harsh winter weather associate as larger flocks in farmland areas. These birds usually prefer to feed on the ground, hopping and walking along in search of seeds. They seek invertebrates almost exclusively for rearing their chicks.

Identification: Has a black band above the bill with grey over the head and neck. The cheeks and underparts are pinkish. The back is brown with two distinctive white wing bars. Cocks are less brightly coloured in winter plumage. Hens have dull grey cheek patches and dark greyish-green upperparts. Their underparts are a buff shade of greyish white.

Distribution: Resident in the British Isles and western Europe, and a summer visitor to Scandinavia and eastern Europe. Also occurs in North Africa. Resident in the west of North Africa and at the south-western tip of Africa.
Size: 16cm (6in).
Habitat: Woodland in parks and gardens.
Nest: Cup-shaped in a tree fork.
Eggs: 4–5, light brown or blue with dark, often smudgy markings.
Food: Seeds and some invertebrates.

European goldfinch

Carduelis carduelis

The long, narrow bill of the goldfinch enables it to prise kernels out of seeds, and these birds often congregate in the winter to feed on stands of thistle heads and teasel. Alder cones are also a favoured food at this time of year. Goldfinches are very agile birds, capable of clinging on to narrow stems when feeding. They are social by nature, usually mixing in small flocks in areas where food is plentiful, although they are usually shy when feeding on the ground. They have a relatively loud, attractive, twittering song. Pairs usually prefer to build their nest in the fork of a tree rather than concealing it in a hedge.

Identification: Bright red face with black lores. Black area across the top of the crown that broadens to a collar on the neck. White extends around the throat, and a brown necklace separates the white on the throat from the paler underparts. Brown back and flanks; otherwise underparts are white. Bill is narrow and pointed. Wings are black with white spotting and yellow barring. Tail is black with white markings. Hens display duller coloration with less yellow apparent.

Distribution: Occurs throughout much of the British Isles and mainland Europe, including Denmark but confined to the extreme south of Scandinavia. Also present in North Africa.
Size: 13cm (5in).
Habitat: Woodland and more open areas.
Nest: Cup-shaped, made of vegetation.
Eggs: 5–6, bluish white with darker markings.
Food: Seeds and invertebrates.

Brambling (*Fringilla montifringilla*): 16cm (6in)
Breeds in the far north of Scandinavia. Overwinters in southern Europe and north-western Africa. In summer, cocks have a glossy, bluish-black head and back, and a black bill. Chest and vent are rusty orange with white underparts and dark grey speckling on the flanks. In the winter, black areas are broken by brown speckling and the bill turns yellow. Hens have greyish-brown plumage and a buff-coloured breast.

Common linnet (*Carduelis cannabina*): 14cm (5.5in)
Resident in western Europe and north-western Africa. Summer resident in the north-eastern areas; absent from much of Scandinavia. A red crown and grey head. Back and wings are brown. Sides of the chest are red, becoming paler on the flanks with a white area on the breast. Hens are much duller with a short grey bill.

Common redpoll (*Carduelis flammea*): 14cm (5.5in)
Occurs in northern Europe, including Iceland, moving south in winter. A crimson red cap and black lores, with streaked upperparts. Red chest fading into white on the steaked abdomen. White wing bar, yellowish bill. Hens lack the red on the chest.

Hawfinch (*Coccothraustes coccothraustes*): 18cm (7in)
Present in Europe, apart from Ireland and much of Scandinavia. Occurs in North Africa. Stout, triangular-shaped, blackish bill that turns yellowish brown in winter. Has black feathering around the eyes and throat. The head is rusty brown with a grey collar. The back is dark brown but the rump is a lighter colour. There is a white area on the wings and the underparts are buff. Hens have a grey area on the wings.

European greenfinch

Carduelis chloris

Greenfinches have stout bills that allow them to crack open seed casings easily and reach the edible kernels inside. They are most likely to be observed in areas where there are trees and bushes that provide nesting cover. In the winter, the European greenfinch visits bird tables, taking peanuts readily as well as foraging in gardens. Groups of greenfinches are also sighted in more open areas of countryside, such as farmland, searching for weed seeds and grains that may have been dropped during harvesting. Pairs often nest two or three times in succession during the summer, and invertebrates are consumed in larger quantities at this time when there are chicks in the nest.

Identification: Greenish head, with greyer areas on the sides of the face and wings. Yellowish-green breast, with yellow also evident on the flight feathers. Relatively large, conical bill. Hen is duller, with greyer tone overall, brownish mantle and less yellow on the wings.

Distribution: Throughout Europe and North Africa apart from the far north of Scandinavia.
Size: 16cm (6in).
Habitat: Edges of woodland and more open areas.
Nest: Bulky, cup-shaped.
Eggs: 4–6, whitish to pale blue with darker markings.
Food: Largely seeds and some invertebrates.

European serin

Serinus serinus

Although mainly confined to relatively southerly latitudes, these serins are occasionally seen in the British Isles and have even bred successfully in southern England. It appears that serins are slowly extending their northerly distribution. Ornithological records reveal they had spread to central Europe by 1875, and had started to colonize France within another 50 years. Serins often seek out stands of conifers, where they nest, although they also frequent citrus groves further south in their range. Young birds are quite different in appearance from adults, being predominantly brown and lacking any yellow in their plumage.

Identification: A bright yellow forehead, extending in a stripe above the eyes, encircling the cheeks down on to the breast. Back is yellow and streaked with brown, as are the white flanks. Hens are duller in coloration, with a pale yellow rump.

Distribution: Resident in coastal areas of France south through the Iberian Peninsula to North Africa and around the northern Mediterranean area. A summer visitor elsewhere in mainland Europe.
Size: 12cm (5in).
Habitat: Parks and gardens.
Nest: Cup-shaped in tree.
Eggs: 3–5, pale blue with darker markings.
Food: Seeds and some invertebrates.

AFRICAN FINCHES

Most of these finches are highly social and are often encountered in large flocks, which can inflict serious damage on ripening crops. Prolific when breeding, these birds are generally short-lived, and studies suggest that they typically have a life expectancy of less than two years. It is not just predators and human persecution that account for this short life span – drought, too, can result in heavy mortality.

Golden song sparrow

Passer luteus

In spite of their name, these birds are not talented songsters, even during the breeding season, uttering little more than a series of chirping notes. Cocks undergo an unusual change at this time, however, as their bills are transformed from a pinkish shade to black. The depth of yellow can vary, being paler in some cases than others and often reflecting slight regional variations. Although golden song sparrows tend not to feed in towns, they frequently roost there in large flocks. They are often nomadic when not breeding, with flocks typically made up of more than 100 birds wandering widely in search of favourable conditions. They breed communally too, and the young are reared primarily on invertebrates.

Identification: Has a yellow head and underparts. Chestnut coloured feathering runs over the back and wings, and merges with black. Hens are a dull brown, and have paler, buff-coloured underparts.

Distribution: Extends in a broad band from Mauritania in western Africa eastwards right across the continent to northern parts of Sudan and Ethiopia.
Size: 13cm (5in).
Habitat: Scrub, cropland and towns.
Nest: Bulky.
Eggs: 3–6, off-white with darker irregular markings.
Food: Seeds and some invertebrates.

Red-cheeked cordon bleu

Uraeginthus bengalus

Distribution: Ranges across Africa south of the Sahara Desert extending to parts of southern Zaire; also occurs in eastern Angola and Zambia. Believed to be present on the Cape Verde Islands.
Size: 13cm (5in).
Habitat: Gardens and grasslands.
Nest: Bulky oval or spherical structure.
Eggs: 4–5, white.
Food: Seeds and invertebrates.

The depth of blue coloration of the red-cheeked cordon bleu varies through its range, especially in the case of males. These colourful finches have adapted well to the spread of human settlement, and are often sighted in villages. They seek food primarily on the ground, hopping along in search of seeds as well as invertebrates, which are used to feed chicks in the nest. These so-called blue waxbills are also sufficiently agile to catch flying ants on occasion. When nesting, pairs are relatively solitary, but after the breeding season, they will reunite to form quite large flocks. The natural environment of these cordon bleus is open country, and although they may wander through their range, they are unlikely to be encountered in densely forested areas.

Identification: Greyish-brown plumage extends from the top of the bill down over the back and wings. The plumage around the eyes down on to the chest and flanks is sky blue, and the abdomen is light buff. Sexes similar except hens lack the dark red ear coverts and also have less blue on their underparts.

St Helena waxbill

Common waxbill *Estrilda astrild*

A highly adaptable species, these waxbills are not only encountered commonly in Africa, but also in other parts of the world, including the island of St Helena where they have been introduced. Other populations are also established on the islands of Rodriquez, Seychelles and Reunion, close to Africa, as well as further afield in locatities as diverse as Hawaii and Brazil. St Helena waxbills are most likely to be observed in flocks in areas where there are relatively tall grasses. Grass seeds feature prominently in their diet. The birds will often roost alongside each other, as well as grasping onto the stems and feeding from ripening seedheads. They rarely stray very far from water. While in proximity to people, whether in gardens or villages, they can become quite tame.

Distribution: Occurs across much of Africa, south of the Sahara. Absent from heavily-forested areas
Size: 12cm (4¹/₂in).
Habitat: Grassland areas and gardens.
Nest: Bulky, pear-shaped structure.
Eggs: 4–8, pink.
Food: Seeds, invertebrates.

Identification: Brown forehead and prominent red eye stripes. They have a pale chest, dark brown, barred wings and heavy barring on the underparts, including the flanks, with slight red markings in the centre of the abdomen. Sexes are alike.

Orange-eared waxbill (*Estrilda melpoda*): 10cm (4in)
From Senegal in western Africa on to the Congo, Zaire, Angola and Zambia. Large, orange cheek patches. Surrounding plumage is greyish but the head is darker. Wings are chestnut brown. The rump is reddish. Sexes generally alike, although hens may be slightly paler.

Silverbill (*Lonchura cantans*): 10cm (4in)
Extends in a broad band across Africa south of the Sahara from Mauritania in western Africa eastwards to Somalia and Tanzania. Also ranges from Saudi Arabia to Oman. The top of the head is dark brown and this continues down over the back and wings. The chest and cheeks are pale buff, but become darker on the abdomen. Silvery bill and black rump. Sexes are similar, but hens may be a little smaller.

Purple grenadier (*Uraeginthus ianthinogaster*): 14cm (5.5in)
Ranges in eastern Africa from Sudan, Ethiopia and Somalia south to parts of Uganda, Kenya and Tanzania. Has a purple area above and below the eyes, and another extensive area of purple on the lower breast over the abdomen and rump. The remainder of the plumage is reddish brown. Hens are much duller with whitish-purple plumage around the eyes and purple elsewhere essentially confined to the rump. Has whitish scalloping on the flanks.

Magpie mannikin

Lonchura fringilloides

Mannikins as a group are relatively dull in colour, with black, brown and white coloration predominating in their plumage. The magpie mannikin is no different in this respect from Asiatic members of the group. It lives in small flocks, but is not especially common through much of its range if compared to other African mannikins overlapping its area of distribution. Tall grasses, reeds and bamboos are favoured roosting, feeding and breeding areas, whether in close proximity to human settlement or further afield. Magpie mannikins seek out ripening seeds, and use their spindly claws to anchor themselves on to narrow stems to obtain food.

Distribution: Ranges from Senegal in western Africa eastwards to southern Sudan and south to Gabon and eastern South Africa.
Size: 13cm (5in).
Habitat: Grassland and woodland clearings.
Nest: Ball of dried grass and similar material.
Eggs: 5–6, white.
Food: Seeds and invertebrates.

Identification: Glossy bluish-black head, and powerful, conical greyish-black bill. Underparts entirely white aside from black and brown barring on the flanks. Back and wings are dark brown, broken by some lighter markings, especially on the back. Rump and tail are black. Sexes alike.

THRUSHES

Various members of this group of birds are excellent songsters, although overall they are not brightly coloured. Their long, powerful bills allow them to prey on a range of invertebrates, and they also feed on berries and fruit. Some thrushes are migratory, either moving within Europe or flying further afield before winter, descending in large numbers in some areas when the weather is unfavourable elsewhere.

Robin

Erithacus rubecula

The robin's colourful appearance belies its strong aggressive streak, for these birds are highly territorial. In the garden, robins can become very tame, regularly hopping down alongside the gardener's fork or spade to grab invertebrates such as earthworms as they come to the surface. Young, recently fledged robins look very different from mature individuals – they are almost entirely brown with dense spotting on the head and chest. Robins are not musical birds, and their calls consist largely of a tick-like call note that is often drawn out and repeated, particularly if they are alarmed by the presence of a nearby predator such as a cat. Since they often feed on the ground, robins can be very vulnerable to these predators.

Identification: Bright orange plumage extends just above the bill, around the eyes and down over virtually the entire breast. Lower underparts are whitish grey, becoming browner on the flanks. Top of the head and wings are brown, with a pale wing bar. Sexes are alike.

Distribution: Resident in the British Isles, western Europe and parts of North Africa. Scandinavian and eastern European populations are migratory, overwintering further south.
Size: 14cm (5.5in).
Habitat: Gardens, parks and woodland areas.
Nest: Under cover, often near the ground.
Eggs: 5–7, bluish white with red markings.
Food: Invertebrates, berries, fruit and seeds.

Song thrush

Turdus philomelos

The song of these thrushes is both powerful and musical. It is heard particularly in the spring at the start of the breeding season and usually uttered from a relatively high branch. Song thrushes are welcomed by gardeners, as they readily hunt and eat snails and other garden pests on the ground. Having grabbed a snail, the birds choose special sites, known as anvils, where they batter the snail against a rock to break the shell and dislodge the mollusc within. Song thrushes can run effectively, which allows them to pursue quarry such as leather-jackets (the larvae of certain species of cranefly). When breeding, they build a typical cup-shaped nest, and the hen is mainly, or even solely, responsible for construction.

Identification: Has brown back and wings, with some black areas evident, and a yellow-buff area across the chest. Dark markings that extend over the chest and abdomen are shaped like arrows, rather than circular. Sexes alike. Young birds have smaller spots and these are likely to be less numerous on their underparts.

Distribution: Ranges widely throughout Europe. Eastern populations head south to the Mediterranean region for the winter. Also in North Africa, even as far south as the Sudan.
Size: 22cm (8.5in).
Habitat: Woodlands and gardens.
Nest: Cup-shaped.
Eggs: 5–6, greenish blue with reddish-brown markings.
Food: Invertebrates and berries.

Common blackbird

Turdus merula

Blackbirds frequently descend to feed on lawns, seeking invertebrates. After rain, earthworms, which often feature prominently in blackbirds' diet, are most likely to be drawn to the surface, and slugs and snails also emerge in wet conditions. In the 19th century, blackbirds were rarely seen in gardens, but today they have become commonplace. They utter a variety of calls and are quite vocal. Cocks are talented songsters, and both sexes will utter an urgent, harsh alarm call. Although blackbirds do not associate together in flocks, pairs are seen foraging together on occasion. As with other thrushes, their tails are surprisingly flexible and can be raised or lowered at will. It is not unusual to see pied blackbirds occasionally, with variable amounts of white feathering among the black plumage. The majority of these birds, especially those with the most extensive white areas, are cocks.

Identification: Plumage is a magnificent jet black, contrasting with the bright yellow bill, which becomes a deeper shade during the winter. Hens are drab in comparison, being brownish overall with some streaking, notably on the breast, and with a darker bill.

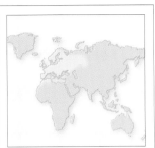

Distribution: Resident throughout most of Europe and North Africa. The majority of Scandinavian and eastern European populations are migratory.
Size: 29cm (11.5in).
Habitat: Woodland, gardens and parkland.
Nest: Well-hidden cup-shaped nest.
Eggs: 3–5, greenish blue with reddish-brown markings.
Food: Invertebrates, fruit and berries

Left: The hen alone is usually responsible for incubating the eggs, although very occasionally the cock may share the task.

Common redstart (*Phoenicurus phoenicurus*): 14cm (5.5in)
Breeds throughout most of the British Isles (except Ireland) and western Europe eastwards into Scandinavia, as well as in North Africa. Overwinters further south in Africa. Has a chestnut-red breast and a black face with a white stripe above. Crown, back and wings are greyish. Has chestnut tail feathers. Hens have greyish-brown upperparts and buff-white underparts.

Mistle thrush (*Turdus viscivorus*): 29cm (11.5in)
Resident throughout most of western Europe south to North Africa. Breeds as far north as Scandinavia and also further east. Relatively large with white underparts, often smudged with an area of grey on the upper breast and displaying a variable black spotted patterning. Pale sides to the head. Grey back and wings. Sexes alike.

Fieldfare (*Turdus pilaris*): 27cm (10.5in)
Occurs in central parts of Europe, overwintering in the British Isles and south to the northern Mediterranean. Has a white eye stripe and grey on the sides of the head. Brown band joins the wings across the back. The rump is grey. Rusty yellow band across the breast with darker markings, especially on the flanks. Underparts otherwise white. Sexes are alike.

Common nightingale

Erithacus megarhynchos

It is often surprisingly difficult to spot the common nightingale, although they often utter their musical calls towards dusk and even after dark on moonlit nights. Their relatively large eyes indicate the fact that these members of the thrush family are crepuscular, becoming active at dusk. Their subdued coloration enables them to blend easily into the dense vegetation, either woodland or shrubbery, that they favour. The common nightingale is only present in Europe from April to September, when it breeds before heading back to southern parts of Africa for the winter. The nightingale repeats the journey north and its arrival is seen as heralding the start of spring.

Distribution: Southern England and mainland Europe on similar latitude. South into north-western Africa. Overwinters further south in Africa.
Size: 16cm (6in).
Habitat: Woodlands, gardens.
Nest: Cup-shaped.
Eggs: 4–5 greyish-green to reddish-buff.
Food: Mainly invertebrates.

Identification: Brown plumage extends from above the bill down over the back of the head and wings, becoming reddish brown on the rump and tail. A sandy buff area extends across the breast, while the lower underparts are whitish. Eyes are large and dark and highlighted by a light eye ring. Sexes alike.

STARLINGS AND SUNBIRDS

These two unrelated groups often show iridescence in their feathering, although not always. In the case of sunbirds, it tends to be confined to cock birds. The iridescence makes the plumage shimmer in the light, revealing otherwise hidden colours. It is thought that the iridescence is linked to the birds' reproductive behaviour, especially as various sunbirds display iridescence only in their breeding plumage.

Purple glossy starling

Lamprotornis purpureus

Like most starlings, the purple glossy is very adaptable in its habits, feeding both in trees and on the ground. They descend to find food in areas after grassland fires, and even grab retreating invertebrates from in front of the flames. Although the traditional nest site of these birds is a tree hole, they have adapted to nesting under the roofs of buildings and even use drainpipes. The hen incubates alone, but the cock bird helps to rear the chicks, which are fed mainly on invertebrates in the early stages after hatching. Invertebrates in the diet help to meet the chicks' need for protein in order to grow rapidly. Outside the breeding season in particular, these starlings can be seen in large groups, made up of as many as several thousand individuals. In such numbers, they readily drive off solitary birds of prey drawn to the colony.

Identification: Upperparts are bluish green. Sides of the face and the underparts are deep purple. Iridescence is most marked on the wings and in the vicinity of the neck. Tail feathers are purple. Iris of adults is bright yellow; grey in young birds. Sexes alike.

Distribution: Extends across Africa south of the Sahara, from Senegal in the west eastwards to parts of Sudan, Kenya and Uganda.
Size: 27cm (10.5in).
Habitat: Light woodland and parkland.
Nest: Sticks in a tree hole.
Eggs: 3–4, blue-green with darker markings.
Food: Invertebrates, fruit and berries.

Splendid starling

Superb starling *Spreo superbus*

Distribution: Occurs in eastern Africa from southern Ethiopia, Kenya, Somalia and western Uganda southwards into Tanzania.
Size: 18cm (7in).
Habitat: Open country.
Nest: Large self-built or lines a tree hole.
Eggs: 4, dark blue.
Food: Invertebrates, fruits and berries.

Like other birds from this part of Africa, splendid starlings roost quietly during the heat of the day, and this means that they are hard to spot in spite of their bright colour. They are most easily observed either early in the morning or late afternoon, often near water. However, these starlings have recognized that tourists are a likely source of food, and they frequent safari camps in some areas. Few birds are more adaptable in their nesting requirements. Pairs may even build in the thatched roofs of village huts or take over the nests of weaver birds, often adding thorny branches around the entrance to give increased protection from predators while the nest is occupied.

Identification: Glossy blackish head merging into shiny blue nape and breast. Distinctive white band extends across breast. Belly is chestnut, and vent and undertail coverts are white. Wings are metallic bluish green. Iris is pale yellowish white. Sexes alike.

Common starling (European starling, *Sturnus vulgaris*): 22cm (8.5in)
Ranges throughout Europe and North Africa. The Scandinavian and eastern European populations migrate south in the winter. Glossy in appearance with purplish-black plumage on the head. Has a greenish hue on the body overlaid with spots, particularly on the neck, back and vent. Dark brown wings and tail. Hens are similar, but their spotting is larger and they have a pinkish rather than blue base to the bill. This distinguishes them from cocks in breeding condition. Young birds are much duller, lacking the iridescence of the adults, and are brownish with a dark bill.

Spotless starling (*Sturnus unicolor*): 22cm (8.5in)
Ranges throughout the Iberian Peninsula and adjacent areas of North Africa. Also found on Sicily, Corsica and Sardinia. Predominantly glossy black with long feathers on the throat when in breeding plumage. During the winter, fine white spotting appears over the head and extends down on to the chest. The bill is yellow but becomes darker in the winter, when the plumage itself becomes greyer. Hens are similar to cocks in breeding plumage, but have shorter neck feathering and are less glossy overall.

Scarlet-chested sunbird (*Nectarinia senegalensis*): 15cm (6in)
Widely distributed through western Africa from Senegal and the Gambia east to Cameroon and the Central African Republic. Has an iridescent green crown and chin and scarlet-red plumage on the throat and breast. The remainder of the plumage is blackish brown and often a lighter shade on the wings. Hens are duller. They have a mottled dark brown throat with yellowish underparts and are brown elsewhere.

Scarlet-tufted malachite sunbird

Nectarinia johnstoni

These distinctive sunbirds are found in mountainous areas of Africa such as Mount Kilimanjaro in Tanzania. Although close to the Equator, the temperature drops considerably at night here. These birds seek flowering plants, which provide them with nectar in open country, and are often seen near flowering protea bushes. They usually occur in pairs or small parties, although cock birds are often aggressive towards each other, particularly when in breeding plumage. The nest may be constructed from a wide variety of materials, and is lined with feathers and bound together using silk from cobwebs.

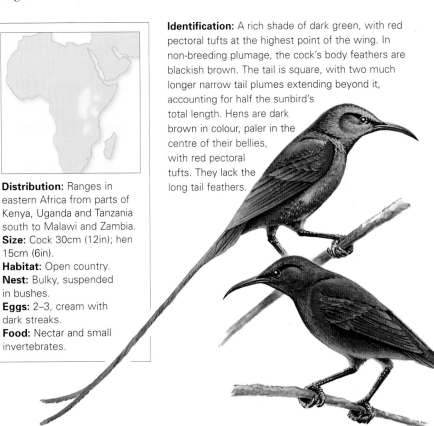

Distribution: Ranges in eastern Africa from parts of Kenya, Uganda and Tanzania south to Malawi and Zambia.
Size: Cock 30cm (12in); hen 15cm (6in).
Habitat: Open country.
Nest: Bulky, suspended in bushes.
Eggs: 2–3, cream with dark streaks.
Food: Nectar and small invertebrates.

Identification: A rich shade of dark green, with red pectoral tufts at the highest point of the wing. In non-breeding plumage, the cock's body feathers are blackish brown. The tail is square, with two much longer narrow tail plumes extending beyond it, accounting for half the sunbird's total length. Hens are dark brown in colour, paler in the centre of their bellies, with red pectoral tufts. They lack the long tail feathers.

Eastern double-collared sunbird

Nectarinia mediocris

There are several different species of double-collared sunbird whose distributions overlap. For this reason, it can be difficult to tell them apart, but much depends on the altitude at which sightings are made. The eastern double-collared sunbird is seen only at relatively high altitudes, above 1,500m (5,000ft), so that it is quite locally distributed through its range. Like other sunbirds, eastern double-collared sunbirds allow a relatively close approach when they are feeding, especially in flower gardens, which they visit regularly. Red flowers hold a particular appeal for them, especially the blooms of red hot pokers (*Kniphofia* species), which are native to Africa.

Identification: Iridescent green plumage on the head, chest and back. The rump is blue. The lower chest is scarlet and has a yellow edging to longer feathers (known as pectoral tufts). The remainder of the underparts are olive. The wings and tail are dark and the bill is relatively short and narrow, curving down at its tip. Hens are a dusky shade of olive green.

Distribution: Ranges in eastern Africa through parts of Kenya and Tanzania south into Malawi and Zambia.
Size: 10cm (4in).
Habitat: Forest and gardens.
Nest: Bulky, built off a branch.
Eggs: 2, pale greenish-white with darker markings.
Food: Nectar and small invertebrates.

GLOSSARY

avifauna: The birds of a specified region or period of time.

breeding plumage: The often brightly coloured plumage that the cock birds of some species adopt before breeding.

carpal: The area of plumage at the top of the leading edge of the wings.

cere: The fleshy area, encompassing the nostrils, located above the bill. Often especially prominent in parrots.

columbiforms: The group of birds that comprises doves and pigeons.

contour feathers: The smaller feathers covering the head and body.

corvid: A member of the Corvidae family, such as crows, ravens and jays.

coverts: The specific contour feathers covering the wings and base of the tail.

cryptic: Refers to coloration or formation that conceals or camouflages.

culmen: The central ridge of the bill.

down: Plumage of a loose texture that primarily serves to conserve body heat.

eclipse plumage: A transitional plumage seen, for example, in the drakes of some ducks, occurring after they have moulted their breeding plumage.

frugivore: A species that eats mainly fruit.

irruption: An unpredictable movement of large numbers of birds outside their normal range.

lek: An area where the male birds of certain species perform courtship displays.

lores: The area between the bill and the eyes on each side of the face.

mantle: Plumage of the same colour occurring on the back and folded wings of certain birds.

melanistic: A dominance of black in the plumage, often in a specific colour phase.

migrant: A bird that undertakes regular seasonal movements, breeding in one locality and overwintering in another.

nidicolous: Refers to the chicks of species that remain in the nest for some time after hatching.

nidifugous: Describes the chicks of species that leave the nest immediately after hatching.

nuchal: Plumage at the nape of the neck.

orbital: The skin around the eye.

pectoral: Of or located on the breast.

precocial: Refers to newly hatched young covered with down and fully active.

race: A geographically isolated population below the level of species, which differs slightly, typically in size or colour, from other races of the same species.

raptor: A bird of prey that actively hunts its food.

ratite: A large, flightless bird, such as the ostrich (*Struthio camelus*), which has a flat breastbone without the keel-like ridge of flying birds.

scapular: Of or on the shoulder.

spatule: Spoon-shaped or spatula-shaped feathers, on the wing or the tail.

speculum: A distinctive patch of colour evident in the flight feathers of certain birds, particularly ducks and parrots.

syrinx: The voice organ of birds, located at the base of the trachea (windpipe).

tarsal: Refers to the area at or below the ankle in birds, as in tarsal spur.

torpidity: A state of dormancy, usually undertaken to conserve energy and combat possible starvation in the face of adverse environmental conditions.

wattle: A wrinkled, fleshy piece of skin hanging from the throat or chin of some birds, or present on the head.

INDEX